INSIDE DONCATRAZ

A PRISON DIARY
VOLUME ONE

LEEKAUTHOR.CO.UK

TWITTER: @LEEKAUTHOR

FACEBOOK/LEEKAUTHOR

INSIDE DONCATRAZ

A PRISON DIARY
VOLUME ONE

BY

CRAIG LOWNDES

LEEKAUTHOR.CO.UK

First Published – 13.03.2016
This edition published 22.10.2018

ISBN 9781530504596

A catalogue copy of this book is available from the British Library.

Cover Design: spiffingbookcovers.com
Printed and bound in the UK

www.leekauthor.co.uk
www.facebook.com/leekauthor
twitter @leekauthor

To those who have stood by me throughout this testing chapter of my life.

Thank you.

My name is Craig Duncan Lowndes, I'm 38-years-old, am intelligent and in good health. I have a loving partner and family and I come from a stable working class background. I am also a convicted fraudster. If I were at a meeting of Fraudsters Anonymous, should there be such an organisation, I would receive a round of applause for that statement. However, I'm not at a meeting of Fraudsters Anonymous, I'm sitting in a 7 foot x 10 foot cell at HMP Doncaster, or Doncatraz, as it is known to its staff and inmates.

I am at the very beginning of a four-year prison sentence for 'Conspiracy to Cheat the Public Purse' or in layman's terms 'VAT Fraud'. Along with everyone else who is spending time in one of Her Majesty's hotels I am going to have a considerable amount of time on my hands, so I've decided to utilise some of that time by recording my day to day experiences inside one of Britain's privately run prisons. As this is my first time in prison, I hope that by recording my experiences it may offer a little insight to those who have never set foot inside a prison and to lay some of the common misconceptions about prison life to rest. I would also like to provide, where possible, some guidance to anyone who may be unfortunate enough to find themselves facing or already serving a prison sentence.

I do not intend to go into great detail about my crime; maybe I'll cover that at a later date. I am, however, going to record my experiences as a first time prisoner; the good and the bad points about the inmates, the staff, the management and the prison system as a whole. I will speak about some of the prisoners that I have met during my time here at Doncatraz. I will share their stories, some funny, some tragic, but hopefully all interesting. I feel it necessary to point out at this stage that everything I relay is only how it has been told to me. I will leave it to you, the responsible reader, to draw your own conclusions as to whether the stories sound believable or not. There will be instances where I have witnessed certain events; these will be recorded exactly as they happened without embellishment. You may also notice dialogue scattered throughout the pages of this diary. In these cases the words are exactly how they were spoken at the time. During my time at Doncatraz I would keep a pen and piece of paper to hand whenever possible so as to accurately record actions and words as they happened. While I am not a great believer in the excessive use of bad language, I have found it necessary when quoting some individuals. I find that this helps to give a greater insight into the person and the situation.

I sincerely hope that you enjoy sharing my journey through the first stage of my prison sentence and that you gain a glimpse into prison life.

Tuesday 4th November 2014

My first sighting of HMP Doncaster was around 6.30 pm on the day of sentencing. I'd been transported directly from Leeds Crown Court to the prison. Luckily for me, or so I thought at the time, Armley prison in Leeds was full to capacity and was not taking any more prisoners. I ended up getting diverted to Doncaster, which is a private prison run by Serco. You may be familiar with the name Serco; it became infamous when it was discovered that the company had defrauded £94 million from the government in a scandal involving the electronic tagging of prisoners.

According to the staff at the court, Doncaster was 'a decent nick' and a far better prison than the state run Armley prison in Leeds, so I was feeling a little happier at this point.

It was already dark as the prison transport approached the prison. Staring out the window of the tiny cubicle I was seated, I could see the walls loom ahead of me. They were at least 20 feet high and made from solid concrete. At the top of the wall was a large roll of even more concrete; it reminded me of a very large oil drum perched on the top of it. The whole place looked very daunting in the fading daylight. There was another thing going in my favour at this point and he was sat in the opposite cell to me on the transport. His name was Chris and was my Co-De or co-defendant; in other words, the man who also had the misfortune to be stood beside me in the dock when we were both sentenced to serve time at Her Majesty's pleasure.

Chris had faired slightly better than me and received a three-year prison term in comparison to my four-year term. Knowing that we were going to the same prison certainly helped to ease the feeling of trepidation.

The transport rolled slowly towards the prison gates and then came to a momentary halt as they slowly rolled open. The transport eased through the gates that slowly closed with an audible and sinister clunk. Now secured in the confines of the prison, the doors on the transport popped open, one by one. There was no need for handcuffs as, now we were inside the prison gates, the prospect of escape were minimal.

We filed into the prison via a single metal door and passed through a scanner pretty much like you would see in an airport security area. As with airports, shoes were to be removed and passed through a separate conveyor belt scanner. After passing through the first scanner, still without shoes, I was instructed to sit on a large boxy-looking chair. Apparently, this was also a scanner that checked if I had anything stuffed in my anal cavity. The mere suggestion made me cringe, but it is a very popular way of getting anything from drugs to mobile phones into prison. The thought of using a mobile phone that had just been pulled from someone's ass was not a pleasant one. I was all clear on that front and was now able to retrieve my shoes.

Scanning complete we were herded into a room with three windowed walls and two metal benches bolted to the floor; it was very much like sitting inside a large goldfish bowl. There were maybe seven or eight of us, all new prisoners, some seated, some standing, wondering what would happen next.

A PCO, prison custody officer, popped his head in the room.

"Food and tea on the trolley outside, lads."

I happened to be sitting nearest the door, so I wandered out to see what was on offer. On a metal trolley were ten plastic plates of food and a couple of flasks accompanied by ten plastic cups and an assortment of plastic cutlery. I took a cup and poured in some very weak looking liquid that I assumed was tea and selected one of the plates. There looked to be two different meals on offer although I could not work out what either was supposed to be. I returned to the fish tank to drink the tea and pick at the food. After eating a few forkfuls of the food I was still at a loss as to what it was meant to resemble. To make matters worse the tea contained so much sugar that my teeth were beginning to itch.

Beyond the fish tank was a large counter behind which stood two PCOs, one of which shouted my name. I gave up on the tea and the food and dumped them on the trolley as I walked past toward the counter. I stood in front of the PCO and waited. He had two plastic bags in front of him containing my belongings taken from me at the court. The two bags were emptied and repacked into things I could keep and things I could not. Items that I was not permitted to take into the prison would be stored until my release or could be collected by a friend or relative upon their visit. The items that couldn't be taken included my suit, tie, court shoes, razor blades, toothpaste and shower gel. I was a bit disappointed – I'd just spent around £30 the day before stocking up on toiletries in readiness for my incarceration.

Again though, Lady Luck was smiling down on me. Normally a prisoner's outside clothing is kept in storage for the first two weeks while prisoners wear the prison-issue clothing. After the two-week period a prisoner is handed back his civilian clothing. It just so happened that the transport that brought me to Doncaster was the last one they were accepting – the prison was now up to its operating capacity of 1,130 prisoners and thus had run out of prison clothing. So my four polo tops, one jumper, two pairs of jeans and one pair of trainers, all Hugo Boss, were put into the 'can keep' bag along with my toothbrush, which they let me keep, four books and some assorted stationery. All of these items were catalogued by the PCO who happened to comment on my choice of clothing.

'Fucking hell, Lowndes, with all this Boss gear you're either a drug dealer or a fraudster.'

I had to confirm his suspicions and admitted to being a fraudster. For some reason I didn't mind being classed a fraudster but 'drug dealer' had an uncomfortable sound to it. The usual questions then followed:

'How much did you swindle?'

And the big one:

'Have you still got any of it stashed away?'

My answer was, and continued to be the same, whenever asked:

'Enough and no comment.'

The two PCOs had a little bitching match about how little money they were paid and that they had to settle with shopping at Primark, not Hugo Boss.

'Who says crime doesn't pay?' replied the PCO.

I felt compelled to remind them that at least they would be going home tonight.

As if reading my mind I heard, 'If you knew my wife you wouldn't swap places with me.' The second

PCO was grinning as he listed the items that I could not take into prison.

I signed a couple of forms and was handed the clothing bag while the other bag was taken into storage behind the counter. The £130 cash that was taken from me at court was to be deposited into my prison account. The whole taking money into prison thing was alien to me and I only knew what I'd read online, which basically said anything from £100–£200 was an acceptable amount of money to take into prison with you. I'd opted for £150, although lunch at a bar outside the court had set me back £20.

The next thing to happen was completely unexpected. The PCO handed me what I can only describe as a welcome pack; a plastic bag containing biscuits, crisps, Polo mints and a couple of chocolate bars. A few other essentials were also handed out and signed for; a plastic plate, bowl, knife, fork, spoon and cup plus toothbrush, toothpaste and soap. Then another bonus, the PCO told me that I could make a phone call.

Before going to court I had done a bit of research online about what to expect when coming to prison. All the sites I'd visited advised not to expect access to a phone for the first few days. So, having a chance to use one within the first hour of coming inside was a pleasant surprise. I called the better half only to learn that my solicitor hadn't bothered to call her despite my instructions when I left him at court. But luckily I could put her mind at ease as to my whereabouts. I think it was at that moment when the events of the day really hit home. A four-year sentence, that's an awful long time to be away from someone whom you've rarely been apart from for over ten years.

Once the call ended it was time for a photo and fingerprinting. My fingerprints were taken digitally via a small pad connected to a computer terminal, the days of black ink and paper long gone. An ID card with my photograph and prison number was issued along with a phone PIN code accompanied by a two-page form entitled 'Phone PIN Form'. At the time I had no idea what these were and no explanation was given. I threw the PIN code and form into the plastic bag along with my other belongings.

Next followed a quick chat with the 'reception buddy' to assess whether I was suicidal or had any issues coping with the fact that I had come to prison. I will talk more about buddies later on. After confirming that I had no suicidal tendencies and I was generally as happy as could be under the circumstances, I was sent back to the fishtank to wait. Chris was already sat there having been through the same routine a few minutes earlier. At the moment we concluded it was 'so far so good', under the circumstances anyway.

The nurse was the next person to pop her head into the holding room.

'Lowndes and Ratcliffe, come with me please.'

We followed her down a narrow corridor to the medical room; I went in first leaving Chris sat on a metal bench, again bolted to the floor. The nurse asked the same questions that I'd already answered at least twice already; was I suicidal, on drugs, alcoholic or homosexual, etc. Once all the boxes were ticked in the negative and a number of forms had been signed, the other questions began:
'What are you in for?' 'How much did you make?' and the favourite 'have you got any stashed?'

In these situations I find it best to play along with plenty of humour; after all, I had just stated that I wasn't depressed so no point acting like it. I was sure time would pass quicker if I had a light-hearted approach to it all. So, after a bit of light-hearted banter I left the medical room and Chris went in for his grilling.

A waiting PCO took me to a side room for a strip search. The thought of a burly PCO wearing rubber gloves and asking me to bend over shot through my mind – thankfully the search was nothing like that.

'Top off first and turn around,' instructed the PCO.

I turned through 360 degrees and was then told to replace my top.

'Trousers and wangers down, same routine,' continued the PCO.

I guessed correctly that 'wangers' were boxer shorts, so I dropped them, turned through another 360 degrees and then pulled my 'wangers' and jeans back up. Job done and my arse was not interfered with – hopefully a sign of things to come.

Back to the fishtank for a few pages of Martina Coles' 'Faceless' before Chris rejoined me on the metal bench. The room had emptied somewhat and there were now only two others with us in the room. After a further ten minutes another PCO entered the room.

'Lowndes, Ratcliffe, let's go.'

I had realized that here in Doncatraz the use of my Christian name or the prefix Mr was now a thing of the past. We picked up our plastic bags and followed the PCO down long corridors and through a series of thick metal doors, some with an additional barred gate. Along the way the PCO made small talk, asking us about our offence and you guessed it, if we had any money stashed anywhere.

'No comment, Gov.'

We arrived at wing 1D, the induction wing for first night prisoners. The sight that greeted me as the door to wing 1D opened was not an unpleasant one. I was expecting long narrow landings of cells maybe four of five high, but this was a large square area with cells on three walls of the ground floor and then repeated again on a first floor level. The middle of the room was carpeted with a couple of pool tables, table tennis and a table football game. The paintwork looked new and the place seemed generally in good order. Just beyond the wing door was a table at which sat a PCO drinking coffee.

We were handed over to the coffee drinker and the PCO who'd escorted us left the wing after first handing over two thin files that I guessed belonged to Chris and I. The coffee drinking PCO lead us over to a cell with an open door.

'This will be your home for the next few days until a space comes up on a wing,' explained the PCO.

Another prison buddy came into the cell carrying two bedding packs which consisted of a flat sheet, duvet cover and pillow, all navy blue; a grubby-looking duvet and pillow, notice here I use the singular. Prison rules state that a prisoner is only permitted one pillow, of which were already on the bed in an untidy pile. Just to clarify, the prison buddies were prisoners who had spent at least three months at the prison and were generally responsible and trusted men who were easily identified by their purple tops with *Buddy* stencilled on the left breast. The prison buddy had a number of roles within the prison but mainly they were there to listen to the concerns of any prisoner who needed someone to talk to. They were not there to judge or give sympathy but were in a position to relate to what a prisoner was going through. The PCO glanced at the grubby duvet and pillow lying on the bunk then turned to the buddy and demanded:

'Get these two some decent bedding and take that shit to those two Scouse smackheads in 201.'

The buddy obliged; that was a bonus. I guessed that PCOs, like most other people, had an inherent dislike of smackheads.

The new bedding arrived, the cell door swung shut with a bang and the lock slid into position. I began to take in my new surroundings for the first time since walking into the cell. It was roughly nine feet long x seven feet wide; on the right-hand side was a metal bunk bed that was bolted to both the wall and the floor. On the left-hand side was a metal writing desk with shelves on either side of the seating position, again bolted to both the floor and wall. To the right of the desk bolted to the wall was a shelving unit, again made of metal. To the left-hand side of the thick metal door was a wash hand basin made from granite and a toilet sat next adjacent to it. Hanging to the side of the toilet was a shower curtain that could be pulled around the toilet to give a small degree of privacy. On the wall opposite the cell door was a three-foot square window that was split into five sections by two-inch thick concrete; the two sections on each side of the window opened approximately four inches. This was another surprise as I was expecting thick metal bars. The window was dominated by a 24 inch flat screen television compete with built-in DVD player and, as if that was not enough in the luxuries department, there was a kettle and a telephone sat on the metal desk. All in all the room was pretty decent. Notice I call it a room; I had decided that cell sounded too prison-like so, throughout my time in prison I decided I would be staying in a room and not a cell. Not just a room, but also a room with a flat screen TV, kettle and a telephone. To be honest, I'd stayed in B&Bs in Blackpool that weren't this well equipped. I opted for the bottom bunk; to me it was the obvious choice with no climbing up and jumping down, although Chris seemed very happy to have to the top bunk – at least we were both content.

We spent the next ten minutes putting on the bedding and rooting out toothbrushes and toothpastes from our plastic bags. Chris set about tuning in the TV; it was pretty basic, around eight TV channels plus three additional channels that showed DVDs, so not too bad on the entertainment front.

We watched an hour or so of television before the door swung open and an unseen person threw something into the sink before closing and relocking the door. I got off my bunk to have a look at what had been delivered. In the sink lay two small cartons of milk, two clear plastic bags containing cereal and two further plastic bags that contained three tea bags, four sachets of sugar, one sachet of coffee and six sachets of powdered milk. I had to admit that it was continuing to be so far so good. One other detail, and this sounds such a small thing, was located a few feet above the sink. It was our own piece of independence – a light switch. I'd always had a preconception that, come 09.00 pm, some unseen prison officer would shout 'lights out' before hitting a master switch that killed the lights. How wrong I was. During that first night I managed to sleep remarkably well and managed a solid eight hours. There were a few shouts and bangs from other prisoners early on but by 10.00 pm all was quiet.

Wednesday 5th November 2015

I slept right through until around 7.00 am, which wasn't bad considering where I was. A bit of breakfast TV, a bowl of cereal and a coffee passed the first hour of my waking day. The prison coffee wasn't the best but was by no means the worst coffee that I'd ever tasted either. I think the strangest things about that first night in prison were; one: waking without Amy, my partner next to me, and two: sleeping in boxer shorts. The boxers made me feel I had less freedom than the four walls around me, although I suppose Chris wouldn't have appreciated me wandering around our very compact space without them.

At 9.00 am, our door swung open although I noticed that none of the other doors were. The PCO who had extended the door directed me to a table that was located at the right-hand side of the wing and Chris was sent to a table on the left. My table was occupied by a guy in his mid-50s whose name tag identified him as Dave. I will only identify officers and staff by their first names and in some cases, when I am repeating something that may be considered inappropriate or for a PCO to say or have an opinion on, I will not use names at all. Dave had an open file in front of him and gestured for me to sit down as I approached the table. He was quite an amenable chap and explained that it was his job to categorize me. All prisoners have to be allocated a category within their first 72 hours of coming to prison as a sentenced prisoner. There are four categories of prisoner, A, B, C and D.

Category A is reserved for the most dangerous and violent offenders for example, murderers, rapists and terrorists; category B is for violent offenders, higher level drug traffickers and most remand prisoners, which is prisoners who have yet to be sentenced. Category C prisoners are lower risk offenders, for example, persons involved in lower level drug dealing or prisoners who have served a portion of their sentence at a category B and have proved they now pose a lower security risk. Finally, category D or open prisons – this was where I was sure I would be winding up in the not too distant future. Category D prisons were for low risk offenders such as white-collar criminals or fraudsters such as prisoners and myself who had been served with long sentences and were now coming to the last year or two of those sentences. Category D prisons were supposed to be a stepping stone or a transition between incarceration and rejoining civilised society; prisoners are not locked away in category D prisons and have a lot of freedom to move around within the prison grounds. Coupled with this is the facility for serving prisoners to have days out of the prison, known as town visits and even overnight stays at home with their families.

In order for a prisoner to be fairly categorised, a standard form such as an ICA 1 form, has to be completed. If you are reading this and have an impending prison sentence, please take special note. The ICA 1 or Initial Categorisation Assessment is a standard form that is used nationally in every prison in order to correctly categorise a prisoner. Instead of trying to explain how the form is completed, I've decided to include a copy of my ICA 1 form in this book – you can see it on the next page. How I managed to acquire a copy of this form I will explain later.

Part 2: PROVISIONAL CATEGORISATION: ALGORITHM

SECTION A

- If determinate sentence—current sentence of 10 years or over
- If indeterminate sentence—a tariff of 5 years or over
- Prisoner was Category A during previous sentence
- Prisoners has been treated as provisional Category A whilst on remand.

Section B

- Previous sentence of 10 years or over
- Current/Previous escape from closed prison, police custody (other than resisting arrest), or escort
- Current or previous serious offence involving:
  Violence
  Threat to life
  Firearms
  Sex
  Arson
  Drugs
  Robbery

(NB: Although one or more offences may be ticked here all are within the same bulletpoint and equate to one tick)

Section C

- Previous sentence of 12 months or more for offence of:
  - Violence
  - Threat of violence
  - Arson
  - Sex
  - Drug dealing or importation
- Current sentence of 12 months or more for offence of
  - Violence
  - Threat of violence
  - Arson
  - Sex
  - Drug dealing or importation
- Within past 3 years:
  - Abscond
  - Failure to surrender
  - Breach of bail
  - HDC or ROTL failure
- Outstanding:
  Confiscation Order
  Further charges
- Serious Crime Prevention Order imposed

PROVISIONAL SECURITY CATEGORY

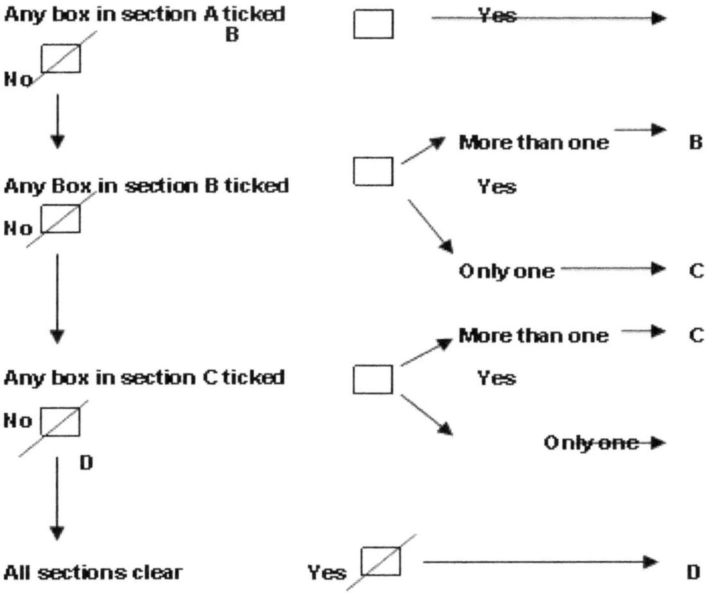

PART 3: ASSESMENT

Are there any circumstances which indicate that the prisoners should be placed in a higher security category than that indicated by the algorithm?

- Security information
- Significant control problem
- Circumstances of offence, pattern of offending
- Identified as Persistent or Prolific Offender (PPO) or facing further charges of a serious nature
- Intelligence indicating involvement in on-going serious crime
- Sentence length. Two years is considered to be the maximum time a prisoner should spend in open conditions. However assessment of a prisoner's individual risks and needs may support earlier categorisation to D.
- Confiscation order, consider whether amount and default sentence imposed might increase risk of abscond

YES		NO	X

If Yes, please give details:

Are there any circumstances which indicate that the prisoner should be placed in a lower security category than that indicated by the algorithm?

- Previous sentence successfully completed in open prison
- Minor offences in section C committed many years ago

YES		NO	X

If Yes, please give details:

RECOMMENDED SECURITY CATEGORY	**D**

Name	**Signature**	**Grade**	**Date**
███	███	Case support	5/11/14

The form was quickly completed and Dave told me that I should be a category D prisoner. He also stated that this was the only logical category for me as this was my first time in any sort of trouble and of the nature of my offence being white-collar. Now, I also feel it is important to point out at this stage that it was not only the opinion of Dave but what the ICA 1 algorithm pointed to. So just to reiterate, the nationally used form used to categorise prisoners, stated that I should be a category D prisoner. Dave then stated that despite the ICA 1 algorithm pointing to a D categorisation and despite his opinion as a categorisation officer being that I should be a category D prisoner; the decision had to be countersigned by his manager. Dave seemed to think that the only problem I may incur was down to the length of sentence. I had been sentenced to four years, which would mean I would serve a maximum of two years in prison. The maximum time a prisoner is normally permitted to serve at a category D prison is 24 months, so I was, as he put it, 'on the borderline'.

'You'll be notified of your category in due course,' Dave assured me. This was a statement that always sticks in my mind. Due course could mean anything from a couple of days or, as it eventually turned out, 11 weeks.

So here I am on day two in a category B prison, sitting my assessment for categorisation and not receiving one. I soon learn that Chris is in the same boat; the nationally approved algorithm had pointed him to a D category but he has a community service breach on his record that occurred four years ago. The ICA 1 state that only breaches occurring within a three-year period can be considered, however, his assessing officer states:

'You should be a cat D prisoner but because of your community service breach, it may be refused by the counter signing officer.'

We returned to our room and were cheerily chatting about the prospects of getting sent to a category D prison when a female PCO by the name of Leah popped her head in and informed us that we were to be moved to wing 1A. The following exchange I am able to recall word for word:

'Is it nice on 1A?' I asked Leah in a jovial tone.

'No, it's an absolute shithole,' she responded.

Just what I needed to hear, but on the plus side, Chris was coming to the shithole with me so it wasn't all bad. We were told to leave the new duvet and pillow but bring along the sheet, pillowcase and duvet cover. We duly obliged and followed Leah down a maze of corridors until we reached wing 1A. As she unlocked the door the first thing that hit me was the noise; it reminded be of being back at school when it was raining and the whole school would have to stay in the gymnasium for the lunch break. We followed her through the metal door, which was immediately pulled to and locked behind us along with the barred gate and across the wing to room 127. Wing 1A was laid out in exactly the same way as the induction wing that we had just left. It was 9.30 am and everyone was out of their cells. We naturally attracted looks of curiosity that any newbie coming onto the wing would receive.

Looking around at the various faces made me feel very old, unless it was just everyone else who was very young; after all, Doncatraz was also a young offenders institute, so maybe that was the reason. We entered our new room and made up the bunks, again me on the bottom and Chris on the top, then unpacked our plastic bags. We were still in the room when a PCO came to the door and stated:

'Exercise or bang up, lads.'

I never learnt this particular PCO's real name but soon came to realize that almost all the inmates referred to him as Sniper, due to the fact that he used to be a sniper in the army, or so the story went. He certainly did not look like an ex-army sniper but then again, looks can be deceiving. If that's not the case Mr Sniper, I apologise; I'm only repeating hearsay.

We opted for exercise as any time spent out of the room had to be a good thing. On balance it was a bad idea, bearing in mind it was early November and I'm only wearing jeans and a polo shirt. Admittedly, it was a very nice and expensive polo shirt but that did not assist in helping keep the cold out. On top of that, the exercise yard was disgusting. Two sides of the yard consisted of the prison building while the other two were constructed of high metal fencing topped with razor wire. The yard was covered in rubbish and was awash with spit. I couldn't understand that, with a population of just over 1100 prisoners, why the management couldn't find two or three trustworthy lads, issue them a couple of bin liners, a litter stick and get this mess cleared up.

We walked around and around that filthy yard for a full hour, which felt more like two. The cold weather didn't help matters. I could have given Sniper a big kiss when he finally shouted that it was time to return inside to the relative warmth. Once back on the wing it was over to the room for bang up. At this point we had no idea how the regime worked and at what times we would be let out to shower, eat or exercise; it was just a case of follow the masses.

When the door opened again half an hour later at 11.30 am, I had a quick look out to see what was happening. I spotted people carrying plates and deduced it was lunchtime, despite the early hour. I gathered my plastic plate, knife and fork and headed out of the room and toward the long queue at the servery. As Chris and I stood patiently in line, various other prisoners simply barged past and proceeded straight to the front of the queue.

Two PCOs were sat at a table located at the front of the wing near the servery and showed no interest whatsoever in the disorderly queue or the prisoners ignoring the queue altogether. I have to admit that to have a young spotty wannabe gangster or girlfriend beater who is half your age barge past you is enough to make your blood boil. It appeared that most of the lads on 1A were not man enough to queue jump on their own, they had to operate in packs of four and five, so to challenge one queue jumper would entail taking on three or four of his mates as well. Not something I was willing to do.

I soon learnt that a large number of the prisoners on 1A were YOs (young offenders, prisoners who are over the age of eighteen but under the age of 21). The YOs all seemed to have an obsession with postcodes. A certain postcode was an association to a certain gang. I suspected that it was probably easier for them to write a postcode when they were defacing a wall rather than attempt to spell out the name of their 'gang'. Most of the rivalry was between 'Donny lads' and 'Sheff lads', but then, throw in a bit of Leeds and Barnsley into the mix and you had a real powder keg. While I'm on the subject of 'Donny lads', I'll share a joke that I heard while I stood in the never ending queue at the servery. I'm guessing that the guy who told me the joke wasn't from Doncaster, as he said it in a very hushed tone, so here we go:

'Why are there so many bakeries in Doncaster?'

'Because they're all in-ter-bread.'

I thought that it was a great joke and the more time I spent at Doncatraz the more I felt it to be a true statement rather than a joke – but I digress. I finally reached the servery and an inmate behind the counter barked:

'Name on pad number.'

'Lowndes, 127.'

'Lowndes, number two,' he said in the direction of the guy stood next to him, who had one hand stuck in the front of his jogging bottoms. With his free ungloved hand he picked up two slices of… well, that was the question; maybe chicken, but then again, maybe pork or turkey, it was impossible to tell, but they were all slapped onto my plate. The next guy behind the counter who, thankfully didn't feel the need to keep one of his hands warm, handed over a bread roll and a packet of crisps. At the end of the servery attached to the wall was a whiteboard beneath which sat another prisoner with a clipboard.

'Choose ya meals,' he said, pointing to the board above his head. There were five options listed for lunch and below that a further five options listed for tea.

'Jacket potato with–' I began.

'Just give me your name, pad number and the numbers of what you want,' he instructed.

'Lowndes, 127, number two and number four,' I replied, my order now placed for the following day's food.

Having received this wonderful lunchtime treat I was now faced with where to sit and consume it.

The tables on 1A were set out in two long rows – it again reminded me of school but this time my first day. Which kids do you want to sit with? Which ones do you feel it's best to avoid? I spotted a couple of spaces and, followed by Chris, headed towards them. As I got closer I spotted a guy chatting away with a mouth full of sandwich; bits of half chewed food dropped out of his mouth and onto the table. On seeing him I decided to carry on walking. At that moment, four black guys got up to have a smoke in the corner so we dropped down where they were seated. Smoking was only permitted in the confines of a prisoner's cell or in the shower room, however, this rule was not adhered to and the PCOs were clearly happy to ignore it. The table was disgusting; it was covered with the remains of other people's lunches. At this point I assumed they were just messy eaters. As I chewed my last bite of sandwich, which I'd finally decided was turkey, one of the PCOs shouted:

'Bang up, two minutes!'

I checked my watch, a cheap thing I'd picked up from Argos, not my customary Rolex. I hated this cheap Argos thing but then again, a Rolex watch and prison were probably not the best of mixes.

The time was 11.52. We'd been out for just over twenty minutes and they wanted to bang us back up.

By 12.00 we were back in the room, door locked, TV on. The door wasn't unlocked again until 4.30; at this time we were let out for tea, so for another 15 minutes we stood in the chaotic queue followed by 15 minutes to eat. At 5.00 pm bang up was called and this time the door would stay locked for 15-and-a-half long hours.

Thursday 6th November 2014

Today would be my first full day on wing 1A. I'd awoken again around 7.00 and started what would be a daily routine of breakfast TV, coffee and cereal. This time the cereal, milk and brew kit was tossed into the sink around 7.30 that morning. The door was supposed to be unlocked at 8.30, but it was actually just after 8.40 when our door was finally unlocked. I noticed lads were walking past our door with plates and heading towards the mayhem at the servery. It appeared that we were the last of the cells to be unlocked. I was interested to see what was being served up at this time in the morning, but soon realized it was only toast. I decided cereal for breakfast would be quite sufficient and I could therefore eliminate at least one queuing session.

As most of the inmates on 1A were sat down eating their toast I concluded that this could be a good time to shower. On arrival, each prisoner is issued with some small sachets of shower gel, soap and a towel that is roughly the size of a pillowcase. Luckily for me, Chris had packed less clothing but two towels, so gave me his spare towel, which was a respectable size. Now, this was one experience that I must confess had played on my mind more than anything else – the prison showers. I hadn't told many people that I was coming to prison, just a couple of close mates who I could trust not to share with the rest of the world. Even though they were close mates it didn't stop them. Whenever they'd had a beer, from going on about prison showers – the usual sort of thing that I would probably be dishing out to them should the situation be reversed:

'If you drop the soap in the shower, leave it on the floor.'

'Don't be bending over to wash your feet.'

'You'll never be short of someone to wash your back.'

Along with many more obscene things that I couldn't possibly put into print. So, I'd formed a mental image of the prison showers, a big steam-filled room with shower heads fixed to the walls at intervals, under which stood big, mean-looking guys who hadn't felt the touch of a woman for years. I was wrong; the shower room consisted of six shower stalls lined along one wall. The sides and door were about five feet high, so the only view of the guy next to you was of his head. Opposite the stalls were three urinals and two toilet stalls, again with five feet sides with a door, so a little privacy was afforded. The one thing the toilet stalls lacked were door locks, possibly the only doors within the prison not to have locks fitted. I was now confident that I could happily bend over in the showers as much as I liked without having to worry about a sex-starved con standing behind me. First thing in a morning also seemed like a good time to get a shower as most of the other inmates were either queuing for or eating toast, so queuing for the showers was something else that could be avoided. I did think it a little odd that there was only Chris and I in the shower room at that time, as apart from the shower room we were in, there was only one other shower room containing a further six stalls on the landing above. These two shower rooms therefore had to cater for the 94 occupants of wing 1A.

It felt good to get a shower, my first one since coming inside, although the tiny shower gel sachets were far from ideal. After leaving, feeling surprisingly clean and refreshed, I went back to the room to drop off my towel. Running through each room, a foot above the floor were two large, cast iron heating pipes; these heated the room and were ideal for draping damp towels over. I also suspected that they would be impossible to rip off the wall or cause damage to.

Back out on the wing Chris and I sat at a table not quite knowing what was meant to happen next; again you weren't told anything, so it was just a case of sit back and wait. The PCOs began to lock the cell doors. It appeared we now had two choices: get locked inside your room or locked out of it; the latter was far more appealing. A couple of lads came and sat down with us, I say lads – one was possibly late

20s while the other was early to mid-50s. We struck up a conversation and apparently these two were in for fraud. Subsequently they had heard that Chris and I were also in for fraud and so decided we all shared something in common.

I was surprised at how quickly other prisoners came to learn exactly what my crime was, after all, this was still only my second day inside and so far the only person I'd spoken to was Chris and vice versa. I guessed the words 'PCO' and 'confidential' didn't go hand in hand. I was not concerned about this, in fact in many cases it's a good thing that PCOs are so loose lipped, but I'll touch on that later. As it turned out, these two were in a slightly different league to us and only knew that we were fraudsters of some description; they had no idea of the type of fraud that we had committed.

The older guy was in for 'taco fraud'. Basically he was a long distance lorry driver who had been fiddling his taco graph so he could work longer hours and therefore to earn extra money. He had received a three-and-a-half-year sentence, which I thought sounded pretty excessive. The younger guy (I will tell his story exactly how it was told to me) had been a carer for his grandfather. Apparently his grandfather enjoyed a bet on the horses but was housebound and unable to make it to the local bookies or to the local bank to withdraw cash to fund his bets. He decided to give his grandson his bank card and PIN number so he could go the bank, withdraw money and place the bets. This went on for just over a year until the grandfather died. At this point the daughter of the deceased man and aunty of the prisoner comes onto the scene and discovers that £20,000 has been withdrawn from her father's account over the past year using the ATM card. As the old man was dead and the facts about placing bets and withdrawing cash could not be verified, the daughter reported the incident to the police and they investigated the matter. As a result the guy gets a three-year prison sentence and here he is chatting to me in Doncatraz.

I had my own thoughts on this story and I'm sure that you will have yours, but in my case they will remain as thoughts and not be committed to paper. To repeat the point again, in this prison diary I am only going to relay stories as they have been told to me. You as a responsible reader may draw your own conclusions and make your own judgements. So, back to the wing, I'm sitting here listening to these guys and, to be honest, feeling a little sympathetic towards them. The older guy had only been sentenced to six months less than me for fiddling his taco so he could work a few extra hours and if he was lucky, earn an extra £4,000–£5,000 over the year, whereas, if you believe the prosecution, I have masterminded a one £1.8 million VAT scam and have lived the life of a footballer, albeit not a premiership one, for the last few years. I must confess that listening to these two made be feel a hell of a lot better about my own sentence.

The younger guy who'd already been in for a couple of weeks filled us in on the daily routine. We'd now be out of the room until 10.00 am; the hour in the morning from 9.00 until 10.00 was known as association, a chance to get a shower and associate with other prisoners, although at this point I wasn't mad on the idea of associating with many of the other people in here. At 10.00 we are then given the chance to spend a glorious hour in the exercise yard or be banged up until lunchtime at 11.30. After half an hour for lunch or less, depending on which order the doors are unlocked, it would be bang up again from 12.00 until 4.30. At between 4.30 and 4.40 precisely we would be let out again until 5.15; this time period was to queue for and then to eat tea and a shower opportunity, should you have time.

That was as good as it got for a possible three hours and 15 minutes out of the room every 24 hours. He said he'd acquired an information leaflet that laid out all the times and that he'd drop one off later on. The information booklets should be located in each cell but in our case we did not have one. I thought at the time that surely it would have made sense to issue each new prisoner with an information booklet at the time that they were issued plates, etc. If there was a good reason why this didn't happen I could not think of it.

The thought of the exercise yard did not appeal so at 10.00 am Chris and I headed back to room 127 for another dose of daytime television. We both tried without success to use the phone that sat on the metal desk in our room. I thought I'd understood the process of making a phone call: firstly dial in the PIN number that was issued at reception followed by * and the phone number, followed by * again. 'Invalid number' was always the automated response. Chris got the same results. As I continued to mess with the phone the door was unlocked and opened by a PCO who was accompanied by a prisoner.

'One of you two Ratcliffe?' asked the prisoner.

Chris jumped down from his bunk and answered the prisoner in the affirmative. The prisoner had come to take him to the weekly meeting of Veterans in Custody. Chris had served in the army ten years previously and was therefore entitled to attend the weekly Vets meeting. I think I failed to mention earlier that at the reception stage all prisoners are asked if they have ever served in any of the armed forces. Chris left the room and followed the prisoner off to the Vets meeting; the door was quickly locked behind him.

After another couple of attempts at trying to use the phone, I remembered the form that had been issued at the same time as the phone PIN number. I sifted through the pile of forms that I had received on my arrival and finally found the 'Phone PIN Form'. Looking over the form I realized that in order to make a call, the number you wished to call was to be added to this sheet and registered. The sheet required the name of the person you wished to add with their full telephone number, address and relationship to the prisoner, for example, friend or partner. There were two sections for adding numbers; one was for social calls and the other for legal calls. I had only brought a handful of numbers with me, so quickly added them to the form. The question now was what to do with this now-completed form? No doubt I'd find out at lunchtime.

Chris returned about an hour later with stories of decent coffee and chocolate biscuits. Cheers Chris, that's just what I wanted to hear. Although on a positive note, he'd got talking to a guy from wing 1B, the wing directly above 1A. This guy Clive had been in Doncatraz for around 16 months and was serving a sentence of 12 years and eight months on a drugs conspiracy. He had told Chris that wing 1A was possibly the worst wing in the prison to be on but that he would have a word with one of the PCOs on

1B that was a very quiet and laid back wing, to get us moved. Apparently some of the staff on wing 1B would cherry-pick prisoners who would tow the line and not cause trouble on the wing. It made perfect sense that a quiet and trouble-free wing would mean an easier life for the PCOs staying on it. We just had to wait until a couple of spaces became available and the right PCO was on duty, although Clive assured Chris that it should not be much more than a week. Happy days.

At around 11.25 am I could hear doors getting kicked and prisoners shouting; it was at least another 15 minutes before our door was unlocked, again, it appeared that we were the last ones to be let out. I was fast realizing that those prisoners who shouted the loudest while kicking their doors were more likely to be let out first than those of us who patiently waited our turn. Again, I suppose the PCOs just wanted a quiet life; if a prisoner 'kicks his doors, let him out, then the kicking will stop', appeared to be the attitude of the PCOs on 1A. I had other ideas on how someone kicking their door should be handled, but that is not the purpose of this book.

I'd ordered jacket potato with cheese and beans. The potato and cheese were eventually obtained from the servery but for some reason the beans were situated on a separate table away from the servery with no means of keeping them warm. When I finally got to the stainless steel container to get them, it was empty. I'm not going to complain about that, as maybe no beans is better than cold beans. What *did* annoy me was, while walking past the rows of tables in search of a seat, I could see piles of beans discarded in the middle of the tables by prisoners who had been let out earlier. This was a common practice for many of the prisoners on 1A when they had finished eating, instead of walking ten feet to the end of the wing to where the dustbin was located. They would scrape any left-over food from their plates and into the middle of the table and, instead of washing their plates up, a slice of bread would be used to give the plate a quick wipe before being tossed onto the pile of food also in the middle of the table. I have to say I've never seen such a disgusting practice, but here in Doncatraz it appeared to be the norm.

I ate my lunch feeling angry at the sheer amount of beans that where discarded on the tables around me. Why the beans were not left behind the servery where they would be kept warm and then evenly dished out, I did not understand. Just as I finished lunch the two-minute warning for bang up was shouted and I managed to collar Leah, the PCO who had fetched us from the induction wing, and ask her what I needed to do with my Phone PIN Form.

She pointed me to a post box fixed to the wall near the entrance to the wing. It was used for anything to do with paper – outgoing letters, phone forms and job applications. Above the post box was another box with the IMB stencilled on it. I wouldn't know how important this box was until weeks later.

As promised, the lad from earlier handed me a prison information leaflet, something to keep me busy during afternoon bang up. After studying the leaflet I learned that for the first two weeks inside, all prisoners were on basic regime. There were three different levels of prisoner: basic, standard and enhanced; I'll talk more about this later. Basic regime meant 21½ hours a day bang up or 20½ hours if you chose to use the exercise yard for an hour. Within the first week all prisoners would attend a two-day induction course, so at least that was something to look forward to. After the first two weeks prisoners could then attend education classes or apply for work within the prison. Each prisoner was only permitted one session of education per day; this was either 9.00 am until 11.30 am or 1.30 pm until 4.00 pm. Prisoners were paid £1.50 per session per day. I didn't fully understand the payments and accounts system until a couple of weeks in, but I'll take this opportunity to run through it now while doing my best to keep it simple.

Each prisoner has two accounts; private cash and earnings. The private cash account contains any money that you had on you when you came into the prison, so in my case £130.00 and, if anyone on the outside sends money into the prison for you it is also added to the private cash account. Each Monday, providing there are sufficient funds, a transfer is made from the private cash account into the earnings account. The amount of this transfer depends on the level of prisoner you are. A basic prisoner gets £10 per week transferred; a standard gets £15 and enhanced prisoners, £25 per week. In addition to funds transferred from private cash are any wages a prisoner earns – as I said, the wages come from attending education or prison jobs. The prisoner can only use funds in the earnings account to purchase items from the weekly canteen; I'll give details about the canteen later. For instance, in my case on Monday, £10 would be transferred from my private account into my earnings account and would be available for me to spend. In order to make telephone calls, phone credit has to be purchased. The credit for the telephone, at this point, is debited directly from a prisoner's private cash account and capped at £50 per day, which I considered to be quite a lot. Accounts balances, phone top ups and canteen purchases are all managed via one of two ATM machines, that are located at the front of each wing.

The ATM looks very similar to the cash dispensers often located within the shops at petrol stations, the ones that charge £1.50 for making cash withdrawals. The wing ATMs are touch screen and are accessed by tapping in a four-digit number that is located on the front of your ID card and then secondly, to verify your identity by pressing your index finger onto a finger print reader located below the screen. The ATMs an actually be used for a number of purposes; visits bookings, phone top ups, booking education courses and canteen shopping. It also allows a prisoner to keep a check on their account balances. The information booklet also informed me that canteen purchases are delivered on a Tuesday and all orders have to be submitted by 6.00 pm Monday. The canteen system allows a prisoner to purchase a large range of products including shower gel, biscuits, breakfast cereals, drinks, stationery and much more. I wasn't able to order anything until Mondays as my money hadn't transferred over until then, but at least it appeared in good time for the Monday evening cut off. Serco prisons used to have a mini ATM in each cell. These would consist of a small touch screen monitor secured to the writing desk. The mini ATMs would enable prisoners to have access to everything that the main ATMs on the wing offered. However, within the first year of the in-cell ATMs being installed at a cost of millions of pounds, they had all broken and were thus unusable.

The afternoons seemed to drag by; four-and-a-half hours of daytime television was a lot to consume in one sitting. It was then that I decided it would be a good idea to start writing, so I began working on a fictional book entitled 'Doncatraz'. Hopefully if you've enjoyed this prison diary you will go on to read it.

At last, 4.30 arrived and we were unlocked to do battle in the servery queue. There seemed to be larger mounds of waste food strewn on the tables at tea time. At 5.00 on the dot we were locked away but I could sill hear other prisoners out on the wing until at least 6.30. To be honest, I was more than happy to be locked away but was curious all the same as to why some prisoners were still out and about.

I have to say and I'm sure Chris would agree, that sharing a room with someone you know and get along with is an absolute godsend. Being able to talk to someone who you are on the same level with was a massive help when it came to passing the time.

Friday 7th November 2015

Friday dragged in much the same as Wednesday and Thursday had. What was interesting was watching the little gangs in the morning association sessions; there would be constant stares and the odd derogatory shout between the factions, but so far, nothing more. Most of the inmates here at Doncatraz and, no doubt in many other prisons, were smokers. As I stated earlier, smoking was meant to be confined to either a prisoner's cell or the shower room, the latter of which I couldn't understand as that particular rule gave no consideration for those of us who didn't smoke and wished to take a shower without a heavy smog heading over us. Subsequently, most prisoners just lit up as they sat around the tables during association and a few of the less refined prisoners would continue puffing away with their roll-ups during meal times. The PCOs on wing 1A seemed more than happy to ignore this practice.

As canteen day was fast approaching I needed to give some thought as to what luxuries I was going to indulge myself with. I decided that first on my list would be a pack of playing cards. There were usually one or two card games taking place during morning association but it was always the same game, prison blackjack. I figured that with my own pack of cards I could perhaps introduce a more interesting and challenging game. My first weekend needed to be endured before I got close to getting my pack of cards.

For some reason, Friday night seemed a lot noisier than the previous nights; loud music could be heard and a lot of shouting between cells. There was one guy in particular who appeared to enjoy spending his Friday evenings balling out of his window. I never got to know his name, but he was one of those people, and most of us know one, who disproves the saying 'you can't judge a book by its cover'. How this guy talked and behaved portrayed exactly the type of guy he was. He never went anywhere unless he had four or five of his mates with him and was one of the main culprits when it came to walking to the front of the queue at meal times. I'll be honest, I never had a cross word or any word for that matter, with the guy, but I just did not like him, which sounds a very shallow thing to say. How can you not like someone whom you've never spoken to? Maybe it didn't help that, one time he ignored the servery queue and would end up with at least two meals on his plate before tipping at least half the food onto the table. A zoo would have been too good for a guy with his table manners, but again I digress. I was also talking about his shouting, so Friday night, from the minute he was banged up (which was usually at least an hour after everyone else until at least midnight) his distinctive and loud voice would boom all manner of uneducated drivel from his cell window. The odd thing was that he would continue despite the fact that no one ever replied to his shouts.

Saturday 8th November 2014

On Saturday the routine changed a little. Our door was opened at around 10.30 am by Leah. I could see lads walking past our door carrying plates yet again, so I asked Leah:

'Is this a late breakfast or a very early lunch?'

'Brunch. We only feed you twice a day at the weekends.'

Brunch consisted of two rashers of bacon or two sausages, a boiled egg, an extremely greasy potato waffle and, if you were lucky, some cold beans that had been stood with nothing to keep them warm for the past 45 minutes. Association then followed until 12.00.

The wing seemed a lot rowdier than it had done in the week. There was a group of lads, maybe in their late teens, sat around a table at the far end of the wing. In the middle of the table sat a large container. It was a 5KG container that would normally hold protein powder to make shakes for body builders. The lads periodically poured whatever was in the container into their plastic prison cups. A Scouse lad who had sat down next to Chris and I piped up:

'Looks like the lads have started early on the hooch.'

Hooch was home-made prison booze made from orange juice, sugar and either orange peel or potato peelings. Yeast or products containing yeast are not permitted in prisons to try and combat the making of hooch, although fermented peel was nearly as effective for hooch production. I thought it sounded pretty disgusting. The surprising thing, or perhaps by now it wasn't so surprising, was how blatant they were about drinking the hooch. There was also loud rap music blasting out of a few of the cells near to where I was seated. At one point two of the lads were stood on their chairs dancing while managing to swill back the hooch, bearing in mind it wasn't yet 11.00 am on a Saturday morning. Was I really in prison or had I been transported to a youth club on some inner city sink estate? I watched in amazement as a lad who was probably in his late teens but looked a lot younger, staggered down the stairs from the top landing; he could hardly stand up despite the early hour. He grabbed four plastic chairs, lined them up in the middle of the association area and then proceeded to lie down across them. The lads drinking the hooch had been watching him since he'd put his foot on the top stair; two of them stood up and moved behind the chairs where the young lad appeared to have passed out. They whipped out the middle two of the four chairs causing the lad to land in a heap on the floor. The two chair pullers high-fived each other before returning to their mates for a great deal of fist bumping and a few more high-fives. The young lad picked himself up and staggered over to the table where the chair pullers were sitting; he swung a punch at one of the guys but missed and fell onto the table.

Finally, one of the PCOs put down his coffee and slowly moved across the wing. The lads quickly placed the container of hooch under the table and hid their roll-ups from sight. The PCO, without saying a word, pulled the young lad away from the table and half carried, half dragged him across the wing and up the stairs to his cell, shoved him through the door and locked it. The PCO returned to his coffee while the lads at the table returned the hooch to its original position and everything carried on.

The sideshow was over so I decided to chat to the Scouse lad; he was in his late twenties and on remand for GBH (Grievous Bodily Harm). His story went something like this:

'One afternoon while I was near my home, minding my own business, two fucking smackheads tried to rob me. Not wanting any aggro I decided to make a run for it. As I was running toward a row of houses I saw an upturned table lying in one of the front gardens. I could hear the lads gaining on me and shouting all sorts of threats so, fearing for my life, I ripped off one of the table legs, turned around and started to knock the fuck out of one of my pursuers. The second guy decided he didn't want the same treatment so he fucked off. A concerned member of the public who had witnessed me getting chased had called the fucking coppers, but when the filth arrived I was holding the table leg and the other guy was lying in a pool of his own fucking blood. So here I am on remand in Donny.'

I have retold that story exactly how it was told to me. As I said earlier, I will try to avoid bad language unless it is completely necessary to get across certain points or to display a certain type of character.

I was fast learning that normally when someone told you their reason for being inside, it was usually because they wanted to hear your story in exchange. I was already getting fed up with telling it, however, so I went for the short version.

'Me and my mate here apparently nicked 1.8 million from the VAT man, but it's all a big set-up, we're completely innocent,' was a response that seemed to satisfy most people.

Some other guy who was listening in wanted to know who the 'VAT man' was and if he was local. I let Chris field that question. That was another good thing from my point of view – Chris was far happier chatting away to other inmates than I was. I'd happily sit back and let him regurgitate the story time and time again and just give the odd nod of agreement here and there. Chris also appeared pretty well versed in prison slang, or maybe it was just me who'd led a sheltered life. I lost count of the number of times that random prisoners would just stop and ask:

'Got any burn?'

Some wouldn't even stop walking, I'd be sat down and they'd ask the question as they passed by. Maybe if someone had the common decency to actually stop, perhaps pull up a chair and introduce themselves, they would stand half a chance. The trouble was I had no idea what 'burn' was. 'Tobacco' Chris informed me, of course. Obvious I suppose, although I'd been expecting it to be called snout. Too many episodes of *Porridge* when I was younger had a lot to answer for.

Being a non-smoker in prison saved a lot of trouble as many prisoners were always looking to borrow burn or a Rizzler, but by borrow they really meant give. My stock answer soon became a blunt 'don't smoke'. This would sometimes cause one of the non-stoppers to at least miss a step. I could see the incomprehension in their faces; 'don't smoke? You're not serious'. Virtually everyone in Doncatraz seemed to smoke, which was another reason why Chris and I were kept together; a smoker and a non-smoker were not permitted to share a cell. There was one particular guy, who obviously didn't hear too well, or maybe he was just stupid, as at least twice a day he would ask for burn. I took to answering him before the words left his lips. As an example, usually when he got near to where I'd be situated, I'd say:

'Don't smoke.'

'How do ya know I was going to ask for burn?'

'Were you?'

'Yes.'

'That's that then.'

Maybe he just didn't recognise me; after all, there were another 92 guys on the wing. So, that was Saturday done and dusted although I still had to endure Saturday night, which was quite depressing. Not depressing in a 'slit my wrists' type of way, of course, I'd just have rather been elsewhere. For the past ten years or so I could not recall a Saturday night when I hadn't gone out. Now here I was locked away at 5.00 pm until 10.00 am the next morning. Chris and I were drinking tea like a couple of pensioners. If nothing else it served to pass the time.

Sunday 9th November 2014

Before coming to prison I shared a couple of drinks with a friend who'd spent a bit of time inside. He'd given me a few nuggets of advice. The one I'd forgotten about until today was 'try and get to church'. He gave me a couple of reasons for this; one: it's apparently recorded on your prison record. Whether that was true or not I have never found out; two: and maybe more importantly, it gets you off the wing for an hour or so.

Getting off the wing for any amount of time was very appealing as a change of scenery was also most welcome. At 9.00 am on the dot the rap music started to boom from more than one cell on the wing that was seriously hampering my enjoyment of Sunday morning's *Bargain Hunt*. I was sure that Tim Wonnacott wouldn't have approved if he knew he was in competition to be heard over gangster rap so early on a Sunday morning.

Finally at 10.40 am, the doors were unlocked and people surged from their cells. I'd already consumed the cereal that had been flung into the sink the night before, so decided to skip brunch. It wasn't as if I was burning off many calories as my daily exercise routine consisted of a walk to the servery and back twice a day. So, I headed straight to the showers, which again were empty with the exception of Chris in the end stall. I wondered when the other 92 inmates of this wing took a shower.

After a lukewarm shower I made a quick detour to the table where the PCOs sat to make an enquiry about church. The PCO looked taken aback by the question; had I asked for a hacksaw and ladder by mistake? No, I concluded I'd definitely asked about church. After a few seconds silence while the PCO debated whether to: ask the audience or take 50/50, he finally decided on ask a friend. His colleague confirmed that church commenced at 11.00 am and I was to 'give him a shout a few minutes before' so he could let me off the wing. The whole process sounded remarkably straightforward. I returned my towel to the room and, as I was draping it over the heating pipes, three prisoners entered the room who appeared very amenable, but I knew I still had to be on my guard. It crossed my mind that they could be a gang of prison rapists come to violate me, or was it that I'd watched *The Shawshank Redemption* too many times?

'You got your telly sorted?' asked one.

'Yeah, it's all good. Cheers,' I replied somewhat defensively.

Their eyes were everywhere; I concluded they weren't rapists but had just wanted an excuse to come into the room to see if there was anything worth stealing. Prison rules prohibited any prisoner from entering any cell except their own, but as I was quickly learning, prison rules were not adhered to on this wing at least.

'Got any burn?' piped up another guy.

'Don't smoke,' was my standard reply, once again.

'What about your padmate?'

'Doesn't smoke either.' With that, they were gone. Not so much as a 'see you later'. Charming.

Chris had replaced them at the door. The situation had not been volatile but it was reassuring knowing that I had someone watching my back and vice versa. I was sure that coming here on my own could have been quite different.

We left the room and joined Taco man and the Scouser for ten minutes while we waited for the allotted church time. At a few minutes to 11.00, the PCO reluctantly left his coffee to walk us the ten feet to the wing door. He unlocked the metal door, then the barred gate and gave us a quick pat down that wouldn't have discovered anything that was hidden on my person, before letting us off the wing and onto the corridor. The gate and door slammed behind us leaving us alone on the corridor; the silence was heavenly. We walked down the corridor until were came to another barred gate, which was manned by a stern looking female PCO who was nearly as wide as she was tall.

'Where you two off?' she demanded in an abrupt tone.

'Church.'

'Are you on the list?'

'What list?'

'You need to be on the list to go to church.'

'How do we get onto the list?'

'You see the vicar.'

'Where's the vicar?'

The PCO stared at me as if I was stupid before replying:

'In the church.'

'Well, can we go to the church, see the vicar and get on the list, please?'

'I'll let you go this once, but in future, if you're not on the list you can't go.'

I wondered if any other religions had this problem. We left the house block and followed the signs to church. We had to walk down two corridors that were long, deserted and very cold. The whole place felt quite eerie. It was clear that few prisoners headed to church, but I was yet to find out differently

The entrance to the church had a barred gate that was locked, beyond which was a solid metal door that was open. The vicar spotted us standing there and moved to let us in. The long chain with the bulky set of keys attached and the heavy-duty boots didn't seem to fit with how one would imagine a vicar to look. However, the crisp shirt and accompanying dog collar was a reassurance that he was in fact the genuine article. The vicar welcomed us into his church and introduced himself as Ozzie; apparently prisoners were even on first name terms with members of the clergy.

'Write your names and prison number on that sheet of paper and I'll make sure that you are put on the list.'

He must have read my mind, or maybe he was just used to hearing the same story from all new prisoners. I must confess to not being a regular visitor to either churches or chapels, but I would describe the prison church as modern. It had a high ceiling with yellow brick walls, together with stained glass windows complete with bars on the outside and a large wooden cross mounted on the wall above the altar table. Church music gently played in the background, although it didn't come from an organ but a couple of speakers connected to a complicated-looking mixing desk. Behind this desk sat a particularly mean looking prisoner with a skinhead and constant frown on his face. There were about 15 other prisoners already seated on plastic chairs, although the front row was completely empty. Not wishing to sit on the front row either, Chris and I selected a couple of chairs four rows back behind a group of five other guys. The service was pretty much what I imagined hundreds of other church services up and down the country were like; a couple of hymns, a Bible reading and, amongst others, the Lord's Prayer. Amazingly, I remembered all the words despite not ever repeating it since leaving school 22 years ago.

The highlight of the service for me was when Ozzie was preparing the table for Holy Communion. Ozzie placed a silver goblet on the altar table, no doubt containing communion wine. The five lads seated in front followed the goblet's every move, their heads moving in unison each time Ozzie moved it. Ozzie announced that we would sing another hymn and then be invited to come forward to the altar to receive the body and the blood of Christ, the wafer biscuit and the wine. As we sung the last words of the hymn the five lads had all taken a step forwards. I couldn't imagine us getting to sip the wine, but maybe these five knew something that I didn't. The hymn came to an end and Ozzie blessed the wine and broke the bread. The five were now learning forward; they were like sprinters on the starting blocks. Ozzie finally invited everyone to come forward and share in the body and the blood of Christ. The five were instantly stood in front of him, while everyone else filed in behind, forming a long but very orderly queue. Ozzie was holding the silver wine-filled goblet, but instead of offering it to the lips of the first prisoner, he simply dipped the wafer into the liquid and placed it into the mouth of the guy. I could see the first prisoner's shoulders slumped in disappointment.

Once back onto the house block, we had a short walk down the corridor to the door that led back onto the wing. I noticed a room on the left with the lights on, the sign on the door stated **Library**. Chris pushed open the door and spoke to a guy sat behind a desk; it was the same guy that Chris had met earlier in the week at the veterans meeting. The guy introduced himself to me as Clive, as Chris said he was called; a very friendly chap probably in his late 40s, who seemed genuinely helpful. We spent a good half hour in the library, which contained maybe 500 books and was only twice the size of our room on the wing. The time was spent just chatting and having a laugh with an Oasis CD playing from the computer sitting on Clive's desk. For the first time since coming to Doncatraz, it didn't feel like I was in prison. As we left the library, Clive assured us that he was on the case about getting us moved off 1A or 'the zoo' as it was also known and that we should be joining him on 1B within the next week or so. That was music to my ears. We made the short walk to the metal door that lead onto the wing; naturally it was closed and locked. At about the same time a prisoner approached the door opposite which lead onto another wing, he gave the door a couple of hard kicks and a few seconds later it was opened by a PCO.

Chris repeated this exercise on our door and again the door was opened and the gate unlocked allowing us back onto the wing. The PCOs were in the process of banging everyone up. As I walked across the wing to room 127, I could hear a banging noise coming from a cell somewhere upstairs. Looking up I could see that it was the one into which the young drunken lad had been thrown into the day before.

'They've had him banged up all day, been kicking off big time,' announced the Scouse lad who was walking in the same direction as me.

Sunday afternoon TV was even worse than daytime TV in the week and the afternoon dragged by. Finally, at 4.00 pm we were unlocked. I won't bore you by keeping going on about the chaos at the servery or the bad food, but I will fill you in about the events during our very first Sunday tea in Doncatraz. From the minute the doors were unlocked the banging noise had started, again from the same cell as before. The drunken lad, I learnt that his name was Josh, was still behind his door and did not like it in the slightest. Quite what he was hitting his door with I didn't know, but it was very loud. From the position I was sat I had a direct view of Josh's door. The glass-covered observation panel that was sat in every door and covered by a hinged metal flap appeared to be cracked; another couple of bangs and suddenly a broom handle smashed through the glass panel. Josh carried on smashing at the thick glass until it was completely gone. I thought that any minute now a PCO would leave their coffee and go up to the cell and sort the guy sort – I was wrong. Now the window was removed, Josh could be heard all over the wing and spent the rest of tea time shouting obscenities though the newly formed hole in his cell door.

Dessert on a Sunday, apparently, was always apple crumble with custard and a very sweet and stodgy apple crumble at that. There was a young looking lad who was sat five or six chairs away from me who had opted not to have the crumble but just take a bowl full of custard. He must have had a friend working on the servery because his bowl was full to the brim with thick hot custard that sat steaming on the table in front of him while he ate his main course. The wing was laid out in such a way that the rows of tables sat underneath the landing of the first floor. Someone walking along the top landing had spotted the bowl of custard sitting on the table below and thought that it would be a good idea to drop an orange from the landing above into the bowl of hot custard. The orange hit the bowl dead centre, propelling thick steaming custard over the table and all over the guy eating his meal. He scooped orange out of the bowl and hurled it at the guy who was on the top landing, who was bent double with laughter. That was all it took to start a full-blown food fight. The only saving grace was that most of the guys had already eaten their food so there wasn't a lot left to throw. Again, the two PCOs stayed exactly where they were, their eyes not shifting from the Sunday papers for a second. Where the hell was I? I never recall seeing anything like this on the old episodes of *Porridge*; by 4.30 pm I was relieved to get locked away.

Monday 10th November 2014

Monday morning came bringing with it one or two small events that would seem unimportant on the outside but inside the smallest things could help to punctuate a normally mundane day. The first thing was that I now had money to spend. Logging onto the ATM I could see that £10 had been transferred from my private account to my earnings or spending account, although it was no longer a full £10 as there were six deductions of 7p. 'Shared daily TV rental' was printed next to each deduction and a further 20p had been deducted labelled as 'Repayment - initial'. I didn't know what this deduction was; I'd ask someone later. Now, in itself it doesn't sound much, but losing 62p when you've only got £10 to spend and many things to buy, is a big deal. I ordered a new razor costing £5, shower gel, £1.15 and a pack of cards, £1. I now had £2.23 left. Chris was in the same situation so we agreed to spend £1.50 each on biscuits, leaving my spending balance at 73p. I used £5 from my private funds to top up the telephone credit. The ATM also enabled me to check if the phone numbers from the sheet I'd completed were on the system; to my relief they were so I could at least make a phone call. A poster next to the ATM gave a guide to call costs; 10p per minute for land lines and 20p per minute for mobiles. Calls made at weekends and after 6.00 pm were around 10% cheaper.

Apart from Josh shouting abuse at anyone who passed by his cell, all was pretty calm. It was during afternoon bang up that I received my first letter. The door opened and a PCO, after confirming that I was indeed Lowndes, handed me a letter. As soon as I saw the envelope I knew that it was a letter from my solicitor. The letter was full of things that I really wanted to hear – I'm afraid I'm being sarcastic here. The letter confirmed that I had been given a four-year sentence, which, in the opinion of my solicitor, was 'excessive but not manifestly excessive' and therefore gave no grounds for appeal. The Crown was now in the process of assessing my assets to see what they could or could not force me to sell in order to repay some or all of the money that I'd defrauded from the state. The one positive about the letter was it stated that, despite my four-year sentence, I would only serve a maximum of two years and, subject to good behaviour, I would spend the last four-and-a-half months on HDC (Home Detention Curfew) or electronic tag, which would allow me to reside at my home address in the UK, but could only be out of the house between the hours of, for example, 8.00 am and 9.00 am, so effectively, I would only be spending 19 months behind bars. Before coming inside I'd also read online about something called ROTL (Release

On Temporary Licence). I wasn't too clear on how ROTL worked exactly, but from what I understood it enabled prisoners to leave the prison for days out, overnight stays at home and the chance for employment on the outside. ROTL comes into force at the 25% point of the full sentence, so in my case after one year. There was no mention of ROTL in the solicitor's letter so I decided that I would have to do my own research on the matter just to clarify how it worked in reality.

Another quite significant thing that I'd read on a number of websites and had also been confirmed by my mate, who had served time, was that prisoners were generally only kept in a holding prison, the prison that you are sent to directly from court, for a period of 28 days. Within the 28-day period a prisoner would be categorised and then sent to a prison that met with the prisoner's category. So in my case, according to a caseworker that I'd met on Wednesday, I should be going to a D category prison, subject to his manager signing it off, of course. Therefore, within 28 days I could look forward to getting moved to HMP Sudbury, a category D open prison that was only 18 from my home town.

For security reasons, prisoners were not told about their moves to other prisons until the very last minute. Normally, a slip of paper would appear under the door the night before the transfer was due to take place, informing the prisoner that he would be moved first thing the next morning before the morning unlock.

When two slips of paper were slid under the door at around 9.00 pm that night, both Chris and I jumped off our bunks; being bottom bunk I was first to the door and snatched up the two pieces of paper. They were cut-offs from an A4 sheet and measured around three inches deep. Along the top of the slip was printed 'Prisoner Movement - Official Sensitive'. I felt my heart rate accelerate – was this it? Could I possibly be moving to a D Category prison so soon, after only a week in Doncatraz? The next line stated Tuesday's date, my name and prison number. My bubble burst when I read the next line:

'Amenities - 9.30 am–11.30 am - Two-day induction'.

Tuesday 11th November 2014

After cereal in the room then a shower in the deserted shower block, it was off the wing to get inducted. I was looking forward to this, as any time out of the room and off the wing was, as you know, always most welcome by me. I headed off in the direction of the church, then followed the signs and found a door marked **Amenities**. I handed over my ID card and movement slip that had come under the door the night before that had caused so much excitement, to the PCO sat behind a desk that was located just beyond the amenities door. He checked my name on a sheet of paper and directed me down a set of stairs to room Red six. Red six was located beyond a set of red painted double doors. On each side of a double width corridor were located four doors. Red six had a laminated sign on it confirming that it was indeed Red six and was the home of **Two-day Inductions**. The room was laid out like a school classroom; a large whiteboard was attached to the wall at the front of the room with a desk in front of it and a few more desks in the middle of the room facing forward. Against each of the other three walls were computer terminals, twelve in total. There was a lady sat at the desk in front of the whiteboard with no one else in the room.

'Lowndes and Ratcliffe?' she asked.

We confirmed that this was correct and handed over our ID cards. She explained that we were to sit a maths and English assessment on the computer.

'It's pretty straightforward, just multiple choice. There's no rush, just try and get one finished this morning and then the other this afternoon,' she explained.

That was two hours for each assessment, so they must be pretty intensive tests; I decided I'd better get a move on. Chris and I sat down a couple of computers next to each other, no doubt there'd be more prisoners arriving shortly. The computer screen gave two options, maths or English. I selected maths first, as I considered that to be my strongest subject. Ten minutes later the computer declared that the test was complete; 'Proceed to next test – Yes/No'. I selected yes and was surprised when the English test began. This one took just 15 minutes before the computer declared 'Test complete'. It was now 10.00 am and still no one else had joined the class; well, maybe induction was specialised and had to be conducted in small groups. I guessed that the test level must go up or something, so decided to relax before moving onto the next one.

Chris completed his two tests a few minutes later and we started chatting about something or other, probably the remorse we both felt about our crime.

'I'm sure there'll be time for chatting when the tests are complete,' said the tutor who sounded exactly like she was addressing a couple of ten-year-olds.

'We've finished.'

'Well, start the next one,' she retorted.

'We've finished the next one too.'

After making a few clicks on my computer she declared that I had a level two in both maths and English. I was slightly disappointed as the highest level was three. Level two was equal to a grade C at GCSE level, so no further education in English or maths was necessary.

After she had assessed Chris' results, she invited us one at a time to join her at her desk. She explained that as soon as the initial two-week period had expired, I would be eligible to start work, so basically a week from today. She proceeded to fill out a job application form for me. I was permitted to make three job choices, in order of preference. She gave me a brief description of the jobs on offer. My first choice was 'Print Shop' as this involved working with computers, followed by 'Catch 22' that involved working with the administration department. She didn't explain exactly what the job entailed, but apparently it was a trusted post and paid decent money, well, decent by prison standards. My third choice was 'Prison Buddy'; this job was voluntary but would look good on my prison record, so it made sense. She went on to tell me that come next Tuesday

I would receive a white slip informing me where I was to report to for work. Great, this gave me something to look forward to, as I was sure that once I started working, the time would pass a lot quicker. I hung around while Chris went through the same procedure; he opted for the same job choices. By 10.30 am we were told that our two-day induction was now complete. We had seriously messed up; instead of enjoying two days off the wing we'd had a little over an hour.

We left the induction room dejected at the prospect of going back to the wing for bang up, however, on entering the corridor I was greeted by a wonderful aroma – food. Opposite the door we'd just exited was a door marked **VT Kitchen**. At the side of the door was a noticeboard displaying a menu alongside pictures of prisoners making pies, cakes, desserts and lots of other fine looking food. We turned around and went back into the induction room. We both changed number one choice of the job application to 'VT Kitchen'.

We arrived back on the wing to be banged up until lunchtime. Lunch and tea followed the same pattern, punctuated by Josh shouting from his still broken window.

Once I was banged up after tea at around 5.10, I made my first phone calls since the first evening I'd arrived. A call to my partner was to be my last for a few weeks, as she was heading back to Tenerife to take care of business and avoid the impending gossip that my incarceration would cause. My conviction had made the local paper seven days after the event and so, what had been for the past 11 months a secret was now firmly in the public domain. It was hard, knowing that I wouldn't see Amy, my partner, for a while. I thought it better to reveal her name as I find the word partner very gender neutral and being where I am, it was pretty important to put emphasis on the fact that I am a heterosexual male. Regardless of the fact that I would miss her, I still felt it would be better in the long run that she was in Tenerife, initially anyway. Leek is where our UK home is located. It is a very small town with some people that have even smaller minds, including one or two who would no doubt be taking great pleasure in my current situation.

The second call was to my dad. The bizarre thing is that throughout the whole episode of getting arrested, the various interviews and finally being charged, the other thing that really bothered me was how I was going to break the news to the old man. As it turned out he took the news pretty well and I suppose that, looking back, he'd already guessed I was up to something not entirely legal. Throughout my business life I had always sailed quite close to the wind.

We discussed him coming along with my mother, to visit, but as Doncatraz was nearly two hours' drive one way for them, I suggested they hang on for a couple of weeks, as I could literally be moved closer to home at any time. We agreed to keep in contact on the phone and see how the next couple of weeks panned out. I have to say that having a phone in the room was a massive thing. I'd had visions of queuing up for a single phone located on the wing somewhere, but this was fantastic.

The only thing that was needed regarding the phone was discipline. Chris would be on the phone at least twice a day; this was a sure-fire way of spending all your money. I had made up my mind that I would be self-sufficient in here and wouldn't ask friends and family to send in money on a weekly basis as many prisoners did. So, I would try hard to limit my phone calls.

At 6.30 pm there was another prison first for me, the delivery of 'canteen'. This was when the weekly 'luxury' items were delivered. This was a big deal for many of the prisoners especially the smokers, who had normally completely run out of tobacco by this point. The PCO instructed me to check that the items in the sealed plastic bag were correct and then to sign a form confirming this. I quickly unpacked my few purchases and decided it was good to indulge in the recently arrived digestive biscuits and a cup of tea.

At around 9.00 pm, just as Chris had begun to snore (and I kid you not, when I say Chris was a serious snorer, it felt as though the whole room was shaking) two sheets of paper came flying under the door. I jumped off my bunk and hit the light. Was *this* the slip informing us of a move to category D open conditions? No such luck.

There were two A4 sheets of paper, one for Chris and one for myself. I passed Chris his sheets as he was now awake and asking:

'Are we on the move?'

'Doesn't look like it, mate.'

The top of the sheet read 'Release date notification slip'. The paper gave details relating to key dates regarding my sentence. Rather than trying to explain I have inserted a copy of the form on the next page.

RELEASE DATE NOTIFICATION SLIP

Offender Copy

HMP & YOI Doncaster

Name: CRAIG LOWNDES

NOMS No: A8343DH Booking No: N81680 Cell: SUI- 1-A-127

Sentence calculated on: 05/11/2014

Sentence(s)

Case/Sentence No.	**Date**	**Sentence(s)**	**Consecutive to**
1/1	04/11/2014	4 Years 0 months 0 days	

Key Dates Non DTO

Number of days in sentence	: 1461
Sentence Expiry Date	: 03/11/2018
Conditional Release Date	: 03/11/2016
ROTL	: 05/11/2015
Licence Expiry Date	: 03/11/2018

For prisoners sentenced before 1 October 1992, the Parole eligibility date shown is the date upon which the first parole review is based. Should you be granted parole your eligibility for actual release will be deferred by any loss of remission or additional days awarded.

If you disagree with any of the above details, please write down what you think the dates should be and hand to your wing office. N.B. Police custody no longer applies for anyone sentenced on or after December 3rd, 2012.

Version: 5.24 Printed: 10/11/2014

09:05

Page 1 of 1

Looking at that single sheet of paper made me realize what a four-year sentence actually meant. If you say four years quickly it doesn't sound long, but 1461 days, which is how it is written on the form, sounded like forever. Now, for law-abiding citizens who are reading this, I'll give a quick explanation of the various dates on the sheet.

Sentence Expiry Date- This is the date, four years after my sentence date and the official date that my sentence ends.

Conditional Release Date- As most of you probably know, a prisoner only serves half of his sentence in prison, so this date is the halfway point at which time a prisoner can leave the prison permanently.

ROTL- (pronounced 'Rottle') or Release on Temporary Licence, this is when a prisoner is permitted to leave the prison for singular days to begin with and then build up to a prisoner spending up to four nights at a time at home. This is a gradual process that is built up over time. In my case for example, my ROTL date is 5/11/15, so on the 6/11/15 the prison, subject to security checks, would allow me to leave the prison at 9.00 am and return on the same day at around 6.00 pm. I could utilise that time to spend with family or attend job interviews. As long as I returned to the prison no later than 6.00

pm the process could then be repeated on future occasions.

Licence Expiry Date- This date is the same as the sentence expiry date. Basically, once released from a prison at the halfway point, the second half of the sentence is carried out in society, which means that you should be a productive member of society and not get into trouble of any description. The slightest breach of licence, from swearing at a police officer to drunk and disorderly, would land you back in prison on what is known as 'recall'. The recall is a minimum of 28 days, depending on the offence.
Something that did not appear on my form but appeared on Chris' was:

HDC Date- Home Detection Curfew or 'tagging'. This date is normally four to five months before the halfway point of a prisoner's sentence. For example, if a person is sentenced to two years in prison they would be required to serve twelve months in prison, however, if that person was eligible for HDC they would be released after only eight months. A prisoner who is subject to HDC is required to wear an electronic tag on their ankle. The tag would regulate how much time a prisoner was permitted to spend outside of his home. The minimum amount of time a prisoner must be in the confines of his own house is eight hours per day. In the past a landline was required and a tracking box would be plugged into the home phone socket, between the hours of, for example, 9.00 pm and 6.00 am as the prisoner's tag would have to be within range of the box. If a prisoner left his house during the curfew time, the box would send a message via the phone line to a control centre and the police would be dispatched to arrest the prisoner. The electronic tag now contains a SIM card and works in the same way as a mobile phone. The curfew times are preset so the prisoner is required to spend 12 hours in his house, but can be adjusted to suit employment needs.

At this point I was feeling a little confused as to why Chris had got an HDC date and I hadn't. Admittedly, my sentence was a little longer, but the letter from my solicitor had clearly stated that I would receive HDC at the 19-month stage. Even my barrister had voiced the same opinion during our chat after sentencing had been passed. If solicitors and barristers don't know the procedure, then we're all in trouble. I put the lack of an HDC date on my sheet down to an administration error; I'd chase it up with someone sooner rather than later. Quite how this would be done I didn't know. I had wrongly assumed that the 'two-day induction' would have covered matters concerning procedures, complaints and general routines.

Wednesday 12th November 2014

The rest of the week didn't change much, with the exception of now having a pack of playing cards. So, now my association time would consist of a few hands of rummy, a far better game than prison blackjack, in my opinion anyway. The card school normally consisted of five players; Chris, the Scouser, taco man, Granddad's bookmaker runner and I.

Josh was still locked behind his door on basic regime, which meant he also had to eat his meals in his cell. The abuse toward other prisoners continued on a daily basis, but getting more vicious and racist as each day passed.

I was really looking forward to the following Tuesday. I couldn't believe how excited I was about the prospect of work, or maybe it was just the prospect of being out of the room for a few extra hours each day. The one thing that struck me during that first week at Doncatraz was how much time I was spending asleep. I'd be asleep no later than 10.00 each evening, sleeping solidly until around 7.30 the next morning and then sleeping an additional two to three hours during afternoon bang up.

Saturday 15th November 2014

Saturday yielded a little excitement when Josh was let out of his cell. All the abuse he'd been dishing out finally caught up with him. Four or five other prisoners jumped on him and issued one serious beating. A beaten and bloody Josh was eventually dragged off the wing by two PCOs. He never returned to 1A, but I did hear later on that he had suffered a broken jaw, so wouldn't be shouting abuse at anyone else for a while.

The usual gangster rap was booming from the usual cells and a few of the younger prisoners were holding a private rave in one corner of the wing. They were no doubt high on something other than the music or the charming prison atmosphere.

The two-hour association period was cut short as usual, ten minutes late getting unlocked and then locked away 15 minutes early. When you are locked away for 22 hours a day, 25 minutes is quite a big deal.

The highlight of Saturday was the packet of chocolate chip cookies that had been delivered on the previous Tuesday. Chris and I had agreed to eat digestive biscuits in the week and chocolate chip cookies at the weekends. Along with a cup of

Nescafé, we demolished a full packet in less than five minutes.

Sunday 16 November 2014

Sunday consisted of a visit to church and I'm happy to report that this week my name was on the list. There was a noticeably smaller congregation this week; maybe the lack of communion wine had dampened spirits.

After church we stopped off at the library. Clive informed us that we should have been moved a few days back but there was a bit of ongoing friction between a PCO on his wing and a PCO on ours, so the PCO on our wing had blocked the move. The PCO on his wing, now rather annoyed that our move had been blocked, was going to wait until the blocking PCO from our wing took a day, then move us to wing 1B and send two YOs down to 1A in our place. YOs or young offenders as I mentioned earlier are generally a pain in the rear end. They all seemed to have something to prove. Prison to them was a badge of honour and no PCO wanted additional YOs on their wing. Our move, according to Clive, was going to take place sometime within the next week. Clive certainly appeared to be very well informed on many matters so I was assured he would be a handy guy to know.

Clive went on to tell us about Josh from our wing. After the two PCOs had dragged him off the wing, they had locked him in the library for his own safety until they had found him a place on another wing. Besides being covered in blood, Josh's eyes had started to blacken and he was unable to speak, probably down to the broken jaw.

Sunday tea time was the usual chaos, but managed to pass without major incident.

Tuesday 18th November 2014

I woke up on Tuesday morning feeling quite positive. It was two full weeks since I'd first arrived at Doncatraz and, according to the lady from induction, today was to be the day that I would start work. As soon as the door was unlocked I grabbed my towel, but instead of going to the showers I first went to the pool table where the movement passes were laid out. A movement pass was needed to get off the wing and also served as a way to inform prisoners where they should be and when. There must have been 40 or 50 passes laid out. I looked over them all twice before conceding that my name was not on any of them. Still clutching to a bit of hope I walked over to the ATM machine, logged in and selected 'timetable'. This option listed the days of the week along with the activity a prisoner had on that day, for example:

Tuesday 18th - 10.00–11.30 – Visit
Wednesday 19th - 9.30–11.30 – Induction

To my dismay there was nothing but blank spaces next to each day on my timetable. With slumped shoulders I trudged to the showers. Maybe tomorrow would be the day.

I don't know what it was but there seemed to be a lot of tension in the air during morning association.

As we played cards, I noticed that the queue jumper and his gang were staring a lot at another small gang of young offenders. Both sides were whispering between themselves, punctuated with the odd finger point. Fortunately, staring and pointing was as far as it got.

Thursday 20th November 2014

There was still no movement slip on the pool table and my ATM timetable didn't herald anything either. I accepted that the chances of starting work this week were somewhere between slim and non-existent.

I'd just dealt a hand of cards when a PCO wandered over to the table saying:

'Ratcliffe, Lowndes, you're moving wings. Five minutes to get your shit packed up.'

We followed him to our room and begun to pack up. I had the distinct impression that the PCO was very unhappy about us leaving the wing, not from any great affection for us, but probably because he knew who would be coming to replace us.

Everything was thrown in two plastic bags in less than two minutes and we exited the room.

'Aren't you going to empty that bin? I'm sure it wasn't like that when you got here!' snapped the PCO.

He was right, of course. The now half-full bin wasn't like that when we arrived. It was now overflowing and surrounded by rubbish. I decided it best not to point this out and if getting the bin emptied gave him a small sense of victory then so be it.

Bin emptied, we followed him to a fire exit at the far end of the wing. He opened it and stood to one side.

'Up the stairs and bang on the next door up.'

We passed through the fire exit and without another word it was slammed to. As instructed, we climbed the stairs and bashed the fire exit directly above the one we'd just left. A few seconds later the door opened and a female officer stood in the open space. Her name tag read 'Emma' and she was smiling; how very novel. It instantly hit me how smart Emma looked compared to the PCOs on 1A, but I couldn't work out why. The uniform was the same: trousers, shirt and heavy boots. Maybe it was just the friendly face.

'Mr Lowndes and Mr Ratcliffe, I presume. Sorry about the delay, we should have had you last week, but-' she left the sentence hanging. It was most refreshing to hear 'Mr' preceding my name.

'Prison politics,' I offered.

Emma continued speaking as she led us onto the wing.

'Exactly. Now, unfortunately I've got to split you up just for today. We've got a space in 227 and one in 223, then all being well I'll have a double cell free tomorrow.'

That was fine with us; it hit me then as to why Emma looked so much smarter - the black tie. The PCOs on 1A opted to forgo the tie and leave the top two or three buttons on their shirts undone. I felt that this gave off a far less smart and casual image, not ideal for a prison officer.

Chris took room 227 and I took 223. Emma informed me that my new cellmate was at work, as she let me in. The place stank of stale smoke and there were tobacco and dog ends all over the desk. Glancing at the sink I saw a couple of pairs of boxer shorts floating there. The heating pipes were covered in damp socks and there was no curtain around the toilet. I was instantly regretting the move. I decided not to unpack, so just turned on the TV and slumped down in the plastic chair to watch David Dickinson advise some old dear to 'go to the auction and get the real deal'. The real deal was something that I had defiantly not ended up with.

An hour or so later the door was opened and my new cellmate entered. He was about six foot tall, thin as a rake and had deep ginger hair. He introduced himself as Jonesy and then proceeded to roll a cigarette. He asked me if I had a light. When I informed him I didn't smoke he said he'd show me a trick. From on top of the bookcase he pulled out a length of cable, possibly a cord from a kettle with the plug still attached to one end, although the earth pin was missing. On the opposite end of the cord were two bare cables. I watched in fascination as Jonesy placed the roll up onto a book that lay on the desk then pushed the plug into the wall socket. He then touched the two bare cable ends together creating a spark. On the third attempt the spark lit up the roll.

'Neat trick, eh?' grinned Jonesy.

I just nodded as he puffed away, filling the room with stinky fog. Jonesy informed me that he worked in the main kitchen that prepared the food for all the prisoners. The main kitchen was in a central location. Once the food was prepared it was loaded onto insulated trolleys, then the wing staff would go to kitchen, collect the trolleys and push them back to the wing ready for the meal service.

'You know about 3A?' he asked.

'No idea, I've only been in a couple of weeks.'

'Where they keep all the nonces, and I get to make up their food.' He let out a loud laugh before continuing. Just to clarify, 'nonce' is prison slang for sex offender and are universally hated by prisoners and staff alike.

'There's one guy on there that is diabetic and we have to make him special sandwiches, so you know what I do?' he asked.

'No idea,' I replied, not wanting to hasten a guess.

'I cover them in sugar.' He let out another loud laugh followed by an unhealthy coughing fit before spitting half a lung into an overflowing ashtray on the desk.

The next half hour before lunch dragged as Jonesy smoked another couple of rolls and coughed up more lumps of phlegm. When the door opened and I stepped out onto the wing, I spotted Chris coming toward me; he began speaking before he got close.

'Can't cope with this, mate. That old guy I'm in with said he doesn't smoke much but he's already smoked his way through six roll-ups since I've been in there. Then he spent at least 15 minutes with his head in his hands repeating over and over that he shouldn't be in here.'

I was about to relay the experience of my own guy when Emma approached us and asked:

'How are you settling in, lads?'

'Not ideal, to be honest. We're both non-smokers and the two guys we're now in with both smoke. Don't want to be a pain in the ass but I don't fancy a night of second-hand smoke,' I replied.

'Can't have that. Leave it with me. I'll move Turner into 223 with Jonesy and you two can have 227.'

Ten minutes later that is exactly what happened. We began by giving the room a serious cleaning. Clive popped his head in to welcome us to 1B and drop off some cleaning products. We spent most of the afternoon sweeping and mopping the floor, spraying and wiping the surfaces and dousing the curtain that surrounded the toilet in odour neutraliser to try and expel the smell of smoke. The good thing was that, during our cleaning session, the door was left unlocked and open. By 4.00 pm the room was clean and we were unpacked. Emma returned to lock the door, although we'd be unlocked again for tea in around half an hour. At precisely 4.30 the door swung open, we grabbed our plates and headed for the servery. The first thing that struck me was the orderly manner in which everyone queued. No one pushed in or walked to the front of the queue – how very refreshing.

The table layout on 1B was also different to that on 1A. Instead of being set out in long rows the tables were set out individually, each surrounded by six chairs. The tables were also a lot newer.

After getting tea from the servery I joined Clive and another guy at a table located near our room, 227. Clive introduced the other guy as Dan; they had known each other for years and had come inside at roughly the same time although their offences were completely different and unrelated. At 29, Dan was a good 18 years younger than Clive but they had grown up while living in the same small town. Dan had only recently been sentenced to three years and nine months for being caught in possession of £13,000 of crack cocaine. At first I thought he'd said £30,000 but no, three years nine months for £13,000. Three months less than what I had received for my part in a £1.8 million scam. I cannot say exactly how the alleged £1.8 million was shared amongst Chris, me and 'other persons unknown' but it was a hell of a lot more than £13,000 or even £30,000. Again, I had to wonder why so many people fancied themselves as drug dealers when the sentences seemed to be so large. Despite Dan only getting sentenced recently, he was due for release on tag or HDC in about three weeks' time. At the time of his court appearance he had already served 17 months on remand. So to do the maths, three years nine months actually meant he would only serve half - 22-and-a-half months, then the final four months on tag, leaving only 18 months. To conclude, that is 17 months on remand, leaving him just six weeks of prison time from his court date. At this point I'd like to clarify a myth. I've heard many times that time on remand counts as double off your sentence. Technically it doesn't. A prisoner serves only 50% of a sentence and the remand time is a deducted from the time left to serve. I'll give an example:

One year spent on remand, waiting to be sentenced.
Four-year sentence given by the court.
Two years to serve (50% of the four-year sentence).
Minus one year served on remand.
One year left to serve from the original four-year sentence.

Hopefully that makes sense. Back to Dan, he was especially looking forward to getting released as, within his first month on remand, his partner gave birth to their first child. The child would be 18 months old when Dan was released.

I had always had a pretty low opinion of drugs and still do but Dan and Clive were genuinely decent people and, due to the friendliness of these two new acquaintances, my first tea time on wing 1B was a very pleasant experience. We chatted, laughed and told stories. We were just four guys sat around a table enjoying life; it didn't feel like prison at all.

Reality soon kicked back in when a PCO bellowed:

'Let's go, gentlemen, to your doors!'

Everyone seemed to comply without issue. Within less than ten minutes everyone was locked away and the wing was silent.

Friday 21st November 2014

The morning routine differed slightly on 1B. The cereal, brew packs and milk were thrown through the door at around 8.00 am, as opposed to the night before and the cell doors were unlocked at 8.30 am on the dot. Again, Chris and I joined Dan and Clive at what would now be our usual table. Clive asked about jobs and education. I filled him in on the induction session and the yellow job application that had been completed. In response, he simply laughed before saying:

'No point submitting just one form in here, you can guarantee that that one is already lost.'

He then took me over to the ATM. Once I'd logged in he navigated through a series of options and selected a variety of things. When he'd finished he informed me that I had applied for an IT course, a food safety course, industrial cleaning and to be a Toe by Toe mentor; I'll come to Toe by Toe later. He repeated the exercise with Chris and then grabbed a pile of yellow job application forms from the rack near the postbox.

'Fill out one form for each job you want to apply for – keeps it simple,' he instructed.

We both filled out three forms, one for each of the three jobs that we had applied for on the single sheet during induction. Once completed, the forms were posted in the postbox. I asked to see if Clive had any idea as to why I didn't have an HDC date on the release papers.

'Didn't your solicitor explain it all to you?' he asked.

'My Solicitor told me in writing that I would be released on HDC (electronic tag) in about 19 months.'

'Well, you should change your solicitor. As from the 1st December 2013, any prisoner with a sentence of four years or over does not get a tag,' Clive replied.

Bloody marvellous! I didn't know what was worse, knowing that I wouldn't be getting a tag or the fact that my solicitor and barrister were a year out of date with this small but quite important fact. I had to ask myself what other aspects of the law they were not up to speed with.

I was quite envious when Clive left the wing at 9.00 am to go to work. I spent association playing cards with Chris and Dan. Dan's job was wing painter along with a character who went by the name of 'Terry Turbo', who passed the time on the outside stripping abandoned factories, warehouses and shops of anything metal, along with consuming copious amounts of amphetamines. Terry once told me that he had stayed awake for three full weeks. Judging by how Terry would dash around the wing, I guessed his system was still full of amphetamines.

The wing painters had the task of sanding down and painting cells when they became vacant. Luckily for Dan, Terry Turbo liked to work alone when flying paint onto a newly sanded cell wall. During the three weeks that I knew Dan, I never once saw him with a paintbrush in his hand.

Dan was also a compulsive gambler and ran the weekly football card. The entry fee was one shower gel (£1.15 from the weekly canteen) with the winner collecting 15 gels. Eighteen football games would be randomly picked from the premiership, First Division and Champions League; entrants would predict either a win, lose or draw for the home team. The winner would be the man with the most correct predictions. The football card helped to make the weekends a little more interesting.

Saturday 22nd November 2014

During morning association I managed to round up five other poker players and, taking the green cloth used to cover the pool tables, I got a very professional-looking poker table set up. We had to settle for matchsticks instead of chips and the empty card box became the dealer button.

Playing poker transported me away from prison for a couple of hours. The six of us could just have easily been sat in someone's living room or in a pub somewhere, minus the booze of course. Between hands, stories were exchanged of crimes committed, bent and distrusted lawyers and of course pleas of innocence. I was fast learning that this prison, no doubt like many other prisons, was packed full of innocent men, or so they believed.

I'll introduce you now to a guy I met at that poker table; he went by the name of 'Bibs'. That is all I ever knew him as. Bibs was in his early 40s and was on remand for breaking a restraining order against his ex-girlfriend. Bibs had 11 children by a number of different women.

As I mentioned earlier, I am not quoting laws or pretending to know anything about religious practices, I am merely recounting what was told to me. Between hands of poker, Bibs informed us that as a Muslim, he was permitted up to five wives at one time. There was however a proviso to this, which Bibs explained as follows: If the first wife is unable or unwilling to perform a certain task or fulfil a need of her husband then he can take a second wife that can, and so on. The theory goes that five wives should be sufficient to serve every need.

At the time of coming to prison Bibs had a wife and a girlfriend of whom the wife was fully aware. He never actually told us what his wife was unable to do that permitted the extra women and we never asked. The girlfriend had taken out a restraining order against Bibs in the June of 2014; again, he never revealed why the girlfriend felt it necessary to have a restraining order issued against him. With the restraint in place, Bibs returned to the family home to be with his wife. A few months later via Facebook, the girlfriend informs Bibs that the restraining order had now been lifted and that she would like to rekindle the relationship. Bibs duly moved back into the home of the girlfriend. All was well until early November when the two have an intense argument over something that Bibs does not want to divulge. His girlfriend called the police and informed them that Bibs was in her house and therefore in breach of the restraining order that in fact was not lifted but was still in place. Bibs was immediately arrested and brought straight to Doncaster. He was remanded to appear before Doncaster Magistrates' Court in eight weeks' time, by which time he will have served the equivalent of a four-month prison sentence. His solicitor has advised him that he will walk from court a free man, in early January.

'I was on Facebook last night telling her what a bitch she was,' spat Bibs.

I was initially stunned and had to ask:

'Facebook! How did you manage to access that from here?'

'I called my brother, told him to log into my account and what to type,' grinned Bibs.

'You know that all calls are recorded in here and that also the police can access your Facebook page?' asked Dan.

'You're kidding? I hadn't thought of that,' replied Bibs, his confidence gone.

'Well, keep it in mind. If the coppers find out or she tells them that you've been harassing her from in here, you'll be in more shit and you won't be walking out of court in January,' continued Dan.

Bibs then informed us that he would ask his brother to delete his account so he wouldn't be tempted to go on it again. No one around the table was convinced that this would happen.

Sunday 23rd November 2014

By now I'd totally given up on the weekend brunch of cold waffle, colder beans and fatty sausage and was happy to stick with a bowl of cereal, although I would join the guys at the table with a cup of coffee while they ate.

Bibs had joined us for breakfast on this particular Sunday morning.

'That bitch has being mouthing off about me on Facebook again, so I let her have it big time last night.'

He obviously hadn't taken in a word that Dan had said to him the day before, so nobody bothered to say anything to him this time. He launched into another rendition of how his girlfriend had lied about the restraining order and how the police should be prosecuting her and not him. Thankfully it was time for church, so Chris and I left the other lads to listen to Bibs.

'Hey brother, you going to church?' came a voice from behind me.

I turned and came face to face with one of the blackest guys I've ever seen. I confirmed that we indeed were off to church. He followed us out the wing and as we walked he recounted how last week the house block PCO would not let him through the gate because he wasn't on the list.

'Fucking racists. Day all fucking racists in 'ere,' spat the guy, who had a very strong accent and was quite difficult to understand. I simply nodded in what I hoped were the right places. All three of us were let off the house block without any problem. The guy continued to rant, or maybe he was just talking and sounded like he was ranting, all the way to the church gate. As it turned out he *wasn't* ranting; it really was just the way he spoke because he sung in the exact same manner. It sounded as though he was giving God a dressing down, not singing his praises, although I'm sure that God would be happy nonetheless.

After the service as we walked back to the wing, the guy complimented the church service.

'Dat was a fucking nice service an dat vica is a really decent fucking bloke.' The way he said it wouldn't have sounded any more menacing if he'd have actually said:

'I wanted to kill everyone at the service and nail the vicar to the cross.'

The guy was actually decent enough. I discovered his name was Austin and was an immigrant from Uganda. Austin stated that he was innocent and shouldn't be here at Doncatraz. According to Austin, a friend had lent him a laptop computer so he could apply for a job, but it turned out that the laptop was stolen and Austin was

therefore charged with receiving stolen goods and was due to appear in court next week for sentencing. He seemed to think that he would end up with a community service order.
Back on the wing it was time for bang up, so I headed back to the room for some more TV.

As was customary at weekends, tea was served early, so the door was unlocked around 4.05 and I headed to the servery queue. The queue was pretty long albeit very orderly; it looked as though we had been amongst the last to be unlocked. A minute or two later Austin joined us at the back of the queue.

'Fucking racists let me out last. Day wouldn't leave a fucking white man till fucking last!' he spat.

What Austin failed to realize or mention was that his cellmate was a white guy and had therefore also been let out the latest.

Over tea, Bibs again sat at our table spending most of the time with his head in his hands.

'Eight weeks, I can't get my head around it. Eight weeks – that's two full months stuck in here,' he complained.

Clive who was sat next to Bibs and serving 12 years and eight months would probably give up one of his vital organs to swap places with Bibs, but kept quiet on the matter. When Bibs finally finished his depressing moaning, Clive lightened the now subdued mood around the table with a story that one of the PCOs had told him last week. Clive repeated it to us as it had been told to him; I shall do my best to do the same.

'Hey Clive, you remember that kid who was in cell 231? Got released a couple of weeks ago. Always acting the hard guy, he used to walk around as if he had a sack of shit under each arm. Well, I was doing the nightly cell check a few weeks back and when I got to his cell there was a towel on the inside of his door covering the observation window. I unlocked the door only to see Mr Hardman on his knees with a mouthful of his padmate's cock.'

Whether the anecdote was true or not we'll never know but it got a big laugh around the table and defiantly lightened the mood.

Monday 24th November 2014

After a trip to the shower I checked the ATM timetable, more from habit than anything else, and to my delight the screen was not blank. 'Monday 1.30–4.00 pm - IT class', announced the text on the screen. It continued throughout the week too. Fantastic! Off the wing every afternoon and more importantly, out of the room.

I was now sure that time would pass a lot quicker. Association ended at 10.00 am, then bang up until lunch was served at 11.30. After that afternoon, bang up would only be from 12.15 until 1.25 when I would be released in order to attend the IT class until 4.00 pm.

The IT room was located next to where the 'two-day induction' was carried out and the class was run by a guy in his 60s by the name of John. John had retired once but had returned to work on a part-time basis in order to top up his pension. There should have been ten of us in the class but in fact there was only four. John explained that this was not uncommon and went on to explain a little more about the course. There were eight modules to complete starting with word processing, then databases, spreadsheets and so on. Each prisoner was allocated three weeks to complete each module. Once a module was started the prisoner had to complete it before he would be permitted to leave the course for employment or begin a different course. This seemed satisfactory and I was happy to spend as long as possible in the classroom, as time in the classroom was time out of the room and away from daytime television. There was also an added bonus: for every session of IT that I attended I would be paid the princely sum of £1.50. So, at the moment that meant £7.50 per week. I made a quick calculation and realized that £7.50 would be more than enough to cover any expenditure I may incur while in Doncatraz, without needing to use any of my private cash.

Tuesday 25th November 2014

Three weeks to the day since coming to prison. The days seemed to have dragged but now, looking back, I had to wonder where the past three weeks had gone. Monday had flown by; it felt like I was hardly locked inside the room now and I knew that today and the rest of the week for that matter would be the same. Cards in the morning and IT in the afternoon. All in all it was pretty good.

Before starting the afternoon IT session, Chris and I crossed the corridor and entered the VT kitchen to check if there was any movement on our job applications. We spoke to a very friendly lady named Bernie, who informed us that as yet we were not security cleared and that there was a large backlog that had to be worked through. I asked what a security check was.

'To check that you are secure enough to work in here. You may be a mad slasher and we've got some pretty sharp knives in here,' was the reply.

My eyes had settled on the sweets cabinet; I could see cheesecake, scones and carrot cake. The lads who already worked in the kitchen were sat around a table eating their lunches. Their plates were loaded with food from the kitchen hot plate with cheesecake sat on the table too – not a stale bread roll or slice of plastic-looking turkey in sight. I could feel my mouth watering; I had to get a job in here as soon as possible.

We entered the IT class to find that the number of attendees had halved. Now the class consisted of just Chris and I. This didn't seem right; there were 1130 prisoners housed at Doncatraz and we had so far had an induction to ourselves and now an IT class to ourselves.

By the end of the session I had worked through the word processing module, so John told me that tomorrow I could take the mock exam and then the real one on Thursday. I decided that if I didn't have anything positive on the job front I would need to seriously slow down, as the last thing I wanted to do was finish the course and end up spending the afternoons locked away in my room.

As we walked back onto the wing a little after 4.30, two nurses were just leaving. I wondered what fun and games I had missed. As there was no one to ask I walked to the room and was locked away for 20 minutes before being let out for tea. Over tea, Clive informed us that someone on the top landing had suffered a 'spice attack', hence the nurses. Being a little on the naïve side, I had no idea what a 'spice attack' was and, to my surprise, neither did Chris. Clive explained to us that 'Spice' is legally used on the outside to relax carp when they are being transported, but if smoked it can have a similar effect to smoking cannabis. The problem with Spice is that it slows the heart rate and in some cases can slow it to such an extent that the heart actually stops beating. Spice falls into the category of legal highs and cannot be detected in the drug tests randomly carried out in prisons. It is therefore a very popular drug for prisoners to take. Clive went on to explain about the profits that could be achieved from dealing in Spice.

An ounce of Spice could be legally purchased on the high street for around £100. In prison it would be sold in pre-rolled joints or by the gram. One gram was enough to make five joints and a joint would be swapped for a half-ounce packet of tobacco costing around £4.50.

This made an ounce of Spice costing £100 in the high street worth around £2500 in prison. Not all Spice was purchased with tobacco; many dealers within the prison would ask their customers to arrange for cash to be dropped off to associates on the outside by friends or relatives of the prisoner wanting the Spice on the inside. All in all it was big business and the dealers on the inside knew they were untouchable; in fact, they would be making far more money dealing inside the prison then they would if dealing drugs on the outside.

'Spice attacks' were not only common in Doncatraz but also in many other prisons up and down the country. As a result, the medical staff and in some cases, hospital staff, wasted many hours dealing with the effects of Spice.

Wednesday 26th November 2014

The rest of the week didn't differ from the new routine – a few hands of cards in the morning and IT classes in the afternoon. There was one exception for an hour that morning, when Clive informed both Chris and I that we were required to attend the monthly Toe by Toe meeting in the library. I had forgotten that Clive had also enrolled us both to become volunteer Toe by Toe mentors. As promised earlier, I shall take this opportunity to explain a little about the Toe by Toe mentor scheme.

Unbeknownst to me and probably to many other people, 47% of serving prisoners, that is around 40,000 adult males, have a reading ability equal to or less than that of an 11-year-old. A prisoner by the name of Shannon, who when he arrived in prison some 20 years ago, was unable to read or write, through various volunteers within the prison service, he was taught those very skills. Mr Shannon believed that every prisoner should be given the opportunity that he was given and, as a result, a charity was formed in his name. The charity was named the Shannon Trust and works within every prison throughout the UK. The Shannon Trust runs a scheme called Toe by Toe, with the help of prisoners who are able to read and write, to offer help and assistance to those who cannot.

The meeting was run by a volunteer named Richard who had been visiting the prison each month and had done so for the past 12 years. Richard explained that as a Toe by Toe mentor, we were not there to teach prisoners to read, but rather we were there to mentor them. Some prisoners would not want assistance with improving their reading skills, but may either require a letter to be read to them or for help completing an application form. As a mentor there could be a wide range of things that we may be asked to carry out. As the meeting came to a close we were issued with an information booklet along with learning materials and a sign for the door to our room, indicating that we were now mentors; this was to enable other prisoners to know where to look should they need any assistance – it was felt that a prisoner would be more likely to approach a mentor directly than speak to a PCO.

That afternoon I ventured to IT and Chris had his first visit. I shall take this opportunity to relay the story that Chris told me after he returned from that first visit.

The visits hall is a large high-ceilinged room, which looks quite like a sports hall in a leisure centre. There is a small servery at one end where visitors can purchase drinks and snacks for themselves and for the prisoner that they are visiting. There is also a children's play area so the young children can entertain themselves while mum and dad get a bit of time alone, or as 'alone' as you can be in a room with 300 other people. The visits tables were low and bolted to the floor, surrounded by four chairs also bolted to the floor. Three of the chairs were covered in red fabric and the fourth covered in grey fabric. The prisoner is supposed to sit in the grey chair while the visitors sit in the red chairs. There is no doubt a sign somewhere that specifies this although Chris did not see it when he made his way to the visits hall and sat down at the table that he was instructed to sit at by a PCO. Instead of sitting in the grey chair, Chris sat in one of the red chairs. His visitors, his partner and her father soon joined him. His partner sat in a red chair and her father took the grey one. Pleasantries were exchanged before the father decides to get some coffees from the snack bar. As he stands a PCO bellows:

'R14, stay in your seat!'

Glancing down at the table the father notices that R14 is in fact his table and realizes that the PCO must be addressing him, so he sits down. None of them are quite sure why the PCO told him to sit down, but as it's the first time they'd been here they decide to do as instructed, then try again in a few minutes. Ten minutes later the father stands again, same PCO, same response:

'R14, last warning – sit down!'

This time though the PCO came over to the table and, addressing Chris's father-in-law, asks:

'Is this your first visit?'

'Yes.'

'Well, you must stay in the grey chair at all times, only visitors can get up.'

'But I *am* a visitor.'

Apparently the PCO was quite embarrassed and Chris was moved to his correct position. I found it to be quite funny, but according to Chris his father-in-law was quite put out. I can see it from the PCO's point of view, as prisoners are permitted to wear their own clothes there is no way of telling who is a prisoner and who is a visitor. Although for the past five years, visitors are now fingerprinted when they come into the prison and again when they leave. Before fingerprinting came into force there was at least one instance of a prisoner and visitor swapping places; the prisoner simply walked out of the prison at the end of the visit.

Thursday 27th November 2014

Terry Turbo had finished painting out a vacant cell and we ended up moving into it. A lick of paint made such a big difference; no postcodes starched into the walls or the word 'Tawn' scrawled in black marker pen over the heating pipes. I had seen the word Tawn scrawled in a lot of places and on a few occasions heard lads say that that was where they were from, but I had never heard of the place. It turned out that 'Tawn' was actually 'Town' and was what people from Barnsley called it.

Despite being well painted, the new room was absolutely freezing cold as one of the windows wouldn't close properly and left a three-inch gap for the wind to howl through. As being moved to a newly painted cell was considered a privilege however, we thought it best not to moan and simply filled the gap with a prison issue towel.

A quick visit to the VT kitchen before IT class confirmed that we were still not security cleared. I was getting a little frustrated by this stage as I wanted to work but couldn't, despite being informed on induction that work would commence the day after the initial two-week period.

Saturday 29th November 2014

Saturday was what was known as a 'black day'. Everyone got them but luckily at nearly the four-week stage, this was my first one. I was in a really low mood and it didn't help that Chris was the same; two miserable prisoners in one small room. I think that it was the contrast that caused it. I'd gone from a week where my morning and afternoons would be occupied, thus being out of the room for a full six hours a day, to now being locked up for a full 22½ hours.

Sunday 30th November 2014

Luckily by Sunday morning I'd snapped out of my mini low and was looking forward to Monday morning. A new addition arrived on wing 1B that morning, the queue jumper from 1A, the guy who spent his weekends balling from his cell window, Mr Red Dressinggown. Although now without a small gang of followers in tow, he wasn't stomping around the wing. He was locked behind his door and would be for the rest of his time on 1B, due to a fight that had occurred on his last wing when apparently, another prisoner had finally tired of him and gave him a bit of a kicking. As Mr Red Dressinggown had been considered the instigator of the fracas he had been moved off the wing to avoid further violent exchanges. As the staff on 1B didn't want him causing problems on their wing and, as a punishment for his involvement in the fight despite being on the receiving end, he was now on a 28-day basic regime. Basic regime, if the staff chose to correctly enforce it, was bad news. The prisoner would spend 23 hours a day locked away, but in reality it was closer to 24 hours a day. All meals would be taken to their cell by a PCO and the prisoner would eat them in his cell. A shower would only be permitted every 72 hours and the only time a prisoner would be permitted to leave was for 30 minutes each day on the exercise yard. If the weather were bad he would remain locked up.

The television should also be removed for the cell of any prisoner on basic regime, but this rarely happened.

Basic regime or 'the beating' had done nothing to quieten down Mr Red Dressinggown. From the second everyone else was locked away, he would yet again begin shouting from behind his door.

Church had a slightly different format today. As well as Ozzie, the vicar, there was a guest speaker who told us about her life before finding God and the enormous difference the church had made to her life. The story was tragic and consisted of drugs, gang rape and attempted murder. The lady who now had God on her side spent a lot of time coming into prisons, talking to, listening to and helping out prisoners. Some people are truly remarkable.

'Dat fuckin' woman ad a fuckin' 'ard life, but wha' a nice woman, eh?' commented Austin with his typical load and aggressive manner as we walked back to the wing.

Again, in order to have a bit more time before returning to the wing we called into the library. Austin didn't join us.

'I 'aint into readin' fuckin' books and there 'aint no fuckin' books for fuckin' black men anyway.'

Anyone passing by and overhearing him would have thought that Austin had just discovered I was sleeping with his wife and not that he was simply declining an offer to visit the library. Maybe it added to his charm. Clive was seated behind the desk in the library and was chatting away with a Scouse guy from our wing and another guy who had an uncanny resemblance to Sideshow Bob from *The Simpsons* cartoon. The guy was obviously foreign but spoke English to a degree. The Scouser was attempting to speak to him. Between a mediocre grasp of English and a heavy Liverpudlian accent, not much headway was being made.

As we returned to the wing there was a very official-looking woman wearing a navy blue trouser suit chatting to one of the PCOs. As we made our way to our usual table, Clive mentioned that she was one of the prison controllers and very influential. In no time, Chris was on his feet and marching purposely across the wing towards the controller. He spoke to her for a couple of minutes then returned to the table grinning like a Cheshire cat.

'What did you say to her?' I enquired.

'I simply asked her a question. I asked her if she thought it expectable that two inmates who would be entering their fifth week of incarceration and desperately wanted to work, were unable to do so because the prison had failed to carry out basic security checks that should have been completed in the first 14 days.'

'What did she say to that?'

'She found it completely unacceptable and would be giving it her full attention first thing on Monday morning.'

Monday 1st December 2014

Monday morning I automatically checked the pool table for a white movement slip and, to my surprise, there was an extra slip for me: 'Food safety, Red 1, 9.00–11.00 am'. Chris also had one that contained the same information. We left the wing at the appointed time in a good mood, knowing that we would now be spending most of the day off the wing.

When we arrived at the food safety class, there was actually more than the two of us in attendance. The tutor explained that it was a two-day course and we should have it completed by the end of tomorrow morning's session. On completion of the course we would receive a level 2 food safety qualification. This qualification was a legal requirement for anyone wanting to work in any type of food preparation establishment and would normally cost between £150 and £200 to achieve on the outside. Prison was looking good so far. At this rate I'd be leaving Doncatraz a very qualified person all at the taxpayer's expense, which seemed ironic as this was meant to be a punishment and not an opportunity. So far in my first month I was on target to achieve a level 2 in word processing and a level 2 in food safety – what would be the next 23 months' yield?

The food safety course was straightforward enough and our tutor, Paula, issued us with notes to take away to read overnight. According to Paula, so long as we read the notes, we should be able to sit the exam the next morning. The course finished promptly at 11.30 and we headed back to the wing for lunch.

I had noticed that on a daily basis there would be new faces appearing on the wing; some would turn up on a Monday and be gone by Friday, or some would be longer term. As stated earlier, for the most part a prisoner did not know when he would be getting moved. It would normally be a case of a slip of paper coming under the door stating that you were on the move the next morning. However, on some occasions a prisoner got to find out in advance. One particular instance of this was a guy named Roy, mid-40s, serving a relatively short sentence for growing cannabis plants. Roy had served nearly his entire sentence here at Doncatraz and was due for release in eight days' time. Roy had been given the heads up that in the morning, with seven days remaining, he would be transferred to a Category D prison. I could not understand the logic here. The first few days of arriving in a new prison is inconvenient for the prisoner – money takes time to transfer from one prison to another and phone numbers and visitor details are not transferred over. All in all it is a lot of upheaval for the prisoner.

It suddenly hit me as to why Roy and no doubt many others were getting treated this way – money.

Doncatraz is a privately run prison, run by Serco, a huge firm with shareholders to answer to, so ultimately any decisions had to be made with the 'bottom line' firmly in mind. I had heard a few prisoners' comments on how difficult it was to leave Doncatraz in comparison to a state-run prison. For a private prison to run at maximum profitability it needs to have maximum occupancy as it gets paid by the government on a per prisoner basis, so from the prison's point of view, by transferring a prisoner to another prison they are effectively transferring around £800 per week out of the prison door – not good business sense. The other financial factor that a private prison will take into account is the prisoner's category. A private prison receives more money for a category B prisoner than it does for a category C prisoner and even less for a category D prisoner. So, once a prisoner is categorised as a D cat the prison is making less money; therefore, if an opportunity arises to house a B category prisoner, they will look to free up a space by transferring the least valuable prisoners – the D category prisoners – which is obviously what has happened in the case of Roy. I have listed below the cost per place of each category prisoner:

Category	**Cost per year**
Male Local (holding prison)*	£40,722
Male Category B	£33,495
Male Category C	£31,096
Male Open (Category D)	£25,183

*This is where prisoners are sent to from court before ending up in their final category.

Source: National Offender Management Service (NOMS)

The category of a prisoner makes no difference to how they are treated by the prison; a category D and category B prisoner are housed on the same wing, eat the same food and are subjected to the same level of security. The only difference is the amount of money that the prison receives for each prisoner. So the more B category prisoners a private prison holds the more money it makes for the shareholders. There are also another couple of little bonuses for the prison if it transfers a prisoner. First is the transport cost– the prison would receive a sum of money to cover the cost of moving a prisoner and I'm sure this would not be done at cost. The second plus side is that once a prisoner is transferred he is no longer the responsibility of, in this case, Doncatraz. If a prisoner were released directly from Doncatraz at the end of his sentence and goes on to commit a crime, the releasing prison would receive a black mark against its name. This never looks good when a private is attempting to renew its tender to carry on running a prison in the future. So, using the case of Roy, once he was transferred to a category D prison, for his last week, he then became their responsibility. If he committed a further crime upon release then Doncatraz would be in the clear.

At the time I did not apply this financial logic to my own situation, if I had I would no doubt have spent less time here and more time in an open prison – but we live and learn. Doncatraz was only a holding prison and as a rule, a prisoner should only spend 28 days in a holding prison before getting moved to their correct category prison. I was confident that I would be on the move soon, despite the fact that I had apparently been categorised to D a whole 28 days ago and as yet had not received confirmation of this. I knew two other people on the outside, both convicted of fraud offences and both sent to open prisons within 14 days. Maybe I'd hear some good news this week.

Tuesday 2nd December 2014

As promised, both Chris and I got to sit the food safety exam in the morning session and by 11.00 am it was completed. We were excused from the class and, rather than going back to the wing, we decided to call into the VT kitchen to see if there had been any movement on the security clearance.

'Have you two got friends in high places?' was Bernie's greeting as we walked into the kitchen.

The controller was obviously a woman of her word. We were now officially cleared for work, two weeks later than we should have been but nonetheless a lot quicker than a lot of other lads who hadn't had the good fortune of bumping into the controller.

'You can start in the morning unless you're not busy now,' continued Bernie.

Busy? Not a chance – anything to spend some extra time off the wing and out of the room. Bernie directed us to the storeroom at the back of the kitchen where we changed into kitchen whites. We were then directed towards two large stainless steel sinks containing a huge pile of dirty saucepans while bowls and various other utensils sat on the adjacent draining board. This area was known as the pot wash or tins and was where all the new guys started. This even applied to chefs starting out in kitchens on the outside.

I took the washing and Chris the drying. We worked flat out until 12.45 until Steve, a guy in his 60s with typical chef's physique and grumpy persona that I suspected was slightly exaggerated, announced lunch. At this point the other five guys, who I hadn't paid a lot of attention to, dashed to the hot plate and began loading their plates. Steve ambled over to the sink where we had just finished the last of the pots.

'Okay lads, you can eat what you want, but if you want three meals, eat your first one then come back for a second and make sure you've eaten all of that before you think about coming back for more. Do not pile your plates high with two or three meals at once as the prison staff get very funny about prisoners eating the same food as them and they have to pay for theirs.' As Steve spoke I glanced over at the hotplate and could see battered cod, cottage pie and pizza. I had to wonder what sort of person would even consider putting battered cod and cottage pie on the same plate – maybe Steve was just making a point.

I selected cottage pie, cabbage, carrots and gravy; it looked amazing, real food. I couldn't believe how much I was looking forward to such a simple meal. As I joined the other lads at a large round table, a scruffy, unshaven guy with his plate piled high, looked at my plate and asked:

'Is that all you're eating?'

He then scraped back some of his cottage pie to reveal a very soggy-looking piece of battered cod.

'Steve would never see it under there,' he continued, with the smugness of a guy who'd just had his sentence quashed.

'You're a dick, Pickford,' said one of the other guys. No arguments there. The usual prison conversation soon began about sentence lengths, crimes committed, stashed money – the usual. One guy even asked me in a serious tone where I had stashed my alleged money. Even if I *did* have a treasure chest stuffed with banknotes, which of course I don't, I was hardly going to reveal its whereabouts to this guy.

After lunch it was more washing-up until around 1.30 when we returned to the wing. Everyone was banged up for the afternoon at this point, but as we had just finished work we were permitted to use the showers before getting locked away for the afternoon. To be honest, it was pleasant to have a couple of hour's relaxation back in the room. Having done very little for the past month the pot washing had tired me somewhat. Chris was snoring within ten minutes and it wasn't long before I felt my eyes closing.

Wednesday 3rd December 2014

Wednesday was my first full day in the VT kitchen. The VT kitchen or Vocational Training Kitchen was a fully functioning kitchen with a servery and dining area. It was run by two full-time chefs and when possible, ten prisoners. The purpose of the VT kitchen was to provide training and eventually a qualification for prisoners. It also doubled as the staff mess where officers and administration staff from the prison could buy and consume their lunch. The staff had to pay a nominal fee for the food that went a small way to covering the cost of the ingredients.

After leaving the wing and then the house block it was about 9.20 before I actually arrived in the kitchen. The first half hour was pretty quiet on tins, so I took the opportunity to have a look around to see how things worked.

Each prisoner had his own section; one guy made quiches, one pizza, one main course; two guys were on the sweets section, another on salads and one more on sandwiches. Chris and I were on tins.

The unshaven cod and cottage pie eater was on the sandwich section; his job was to make up six packs of sandwiches, each pack containing two sandwiches, therefore a total of 24 slices of buttered bread with various fillings of ham salad, cheese and tomato or plain salad. Somehow he could stretch this task out for a full two-and-a-half hours; how this was possible I would never know.

Next to the sandwich maker was the salad section that was manned by a young black guy in his late teens that had an obsession for older white women. I won't mention his name as he is in a long-term relationship. The guy was like a dog on heat, he'd even get excited as he recounted old conquests. He would chop up a couple of tomatoes then stroll over to the sink where I'd be washing up, then after taking a look around to check no one was listening, he'd begin detailing one of his many conquests.

'Did I tell you when I had my mate's mum?' Without waiting for me to answer he told me, 'We were cruising round one Friday night and I needed to take a shit. My mate said I could use his toilet, so he dropped me off at his house, well, his mum's house and told me he'd come back later to pick me up. I walked into the house, found the bathroom, took a shit then, feeling a bit horny I decided to walk into his mum's room. She was laying in her bed, man, just staring at me, so I thought 'fuck it' and dropped my trousers. She pulled back the duvet and, my God, I shit you not, she was a real hottie – so I dived in.'

He was really getting into the story now, his voice raising a few octaves while he was thrusting his hips to and thro as he spoke. I was struggling to suppress my laughter, as Bernie was now stood behind him.

'She was loving it, man. Hotties drive me crazy,' he continued, almost panting as his eyes rolled back in his head. I thought that at this rate he was going to need a change of underwear very soon.

'What exactly was she loving?' asked Bernie from over his shoulder. She knew full well but wanted to embarrass the guy to the maximum. The colour drained from his face and he slowly turned to face Bernie.

'Get back to your salads, stud,' she said, and then walked away.

He gave a massive white-toothed grin.

'Bet Bernie could teach me more than cookery.'

'You're a bad man,' I replied.

'Hotties love a bad man,' he shot back before returning to his section to chop half a lettuce before heading to the sweets section to give the guys a rendition of yet another hottie who had enjoyed the pleasure of his company in bed. How true these stories were, I would never know, but the way they were told certainly brightened up the day.

After another wonderful lunch and, I must confess, three desserts (the VT kitchen was not going to do my waistline any favours) Chris and I walked past the IT class and noticed it was empty apart from John the tutor, so we called in.

'How's it going, John, bit quiet today?'

'I should have ten in again today, but this is the third day that no one has turned up,' he replied.

'Any chance we could come here for the afternoon session? We finish VT kitchen at 1.30, so the timing would work and we could work on some more modules,' I enquired.

'If it was down to me you could, but as VT kitchen is classed as education and the prison will only permit one education session per day, I doubt the powers that be will allow it.'

'We don't want paying, if that's the problem, just something to keep us busy.'

'In the eyes of the management, if you came in here in the afternoon then you could be taking up someone else's place, and as you can see they're queuing out the door to join this class.' John waved his hand at the empty classroom. What a wonderful system – last week there were only two in a class meant for ten and, this week, no one at all in the class, while here we were wanting to expand our knowledge of computers and use our time productively but unable to do so. I would be interested to see when the class finally did get some pupils.

Thursday 4th December 2014

Thursday and Friday followed pretty much the same pattern – most of the morning stood at the sink in the VT kitchen, which was punctuated by stories from the young black guy; once I got to know him better I christened him The Black Shagger. From here on in I shall use this new name for him.

The Black Shagger, at 19-years-old, already had five children and had decided that once released he was going to start work on the next five.

On some occasions, The Black Shagger would be over at the sink telling a sex story then he seemed to tag with the unshaven guy who would take his place and bore me with a story about stolen Land Rovers. The sex stories were far more interesting and better told.

The other lads in the kitchen seemed to keep their heads down and just get on with their work. I had already decided that if I were moved to salads or sandwiches it would be time to quit; I couldn't understand why two people were needed to do these simple tasks. My aim was to get onto the sweets section, but that would no doubt be a long way off. I may even get moved to another prison before that opportunity arose. Although, even if I was here for a while, it was down to Steve to allocate who was working where. Steve was effectively in charge, he was the tutor/head chef and Bernie was the teaching assistant/assistant chef – tough in reality, however, Steve treated Bernie as an equal. Steve did his best to come across as the grumpy 'I'm the boss' type and Bernie would always appear to be friendly and laid back, but I had the feeling that when it came to the crunch, Bernie would be the one with the serious bite. Both Bernie and Steve were ex-RAF chefs and had plenty of stories to share from their days in the forces; this was probably also the reason that they had such a good working relationship.

John's IT class remained empty on both the Thursday and Friday. We still called in as he too was ex-forces and always had a good story or two to tell. There were a lot of staff at Doncatraz who were ex-forces, although in my opinion the prison didn't seem to have the discipline that ex-forces would be drawn to. From talking to other inmates I had gathered that state-run prisons seemed to be more suited to ex-forces personnel. Maybe after years of discipline in the forces, working at Doncatraz was just a complete change of direction.

Saturday 6th December 2014

Saturday morning we were on the move, not to another prison but to another room, our fifth in just over a month. Room 201, as well as being bloody freezing again, was a television dead spot. Each cell had an aerial socket that would provide prisoners with eight TV channels and three DVD channels; the number of channels could be significantly increased if a prisoner made a bespoke aerial. A prison aerial was made by cutting the end off the aerial cable and then stripping back the plastic covering to expose the copper wire. This was then made into a loop and taped to the window, which would roughly gain access to eighty TV and radio channels, including babe station. I kid you not. Here we were locked up in a B category prison and able to watch babe station on our very own flat screen televisions. Whatever would the 'Daily Mail' think about that?

Most men and possibly some women reading this will know that babe station is a pornographic television station and is a pay-per-view, costing around £20 per month. You will be pleased to learn that the British taxpayer is not funding this particular service. In the case of Doncatraz, someone on the outside usually pays the £20 subscription. Once the payment is made a six-digit code is sent to the mobile phone of the person making the payment. This six-digit code is then passed on to the prisoner on the inside. A wildfire has nothing on the speed that a new PIN code for babe station spreads around a wing. It is a truly amazing thing to witness when someone receives the new PIN; within less than a minute all 94 occupants of the wing are in possession of the coveted babe station PIN code.

Again, I've side-tracked… We were moving out of room 201 partly because it was a TV dead spot and we were unable to pick up any of the extra channels. Our new room was on millionaires' row, the penthouse cells. These were located on the upper landing with a view of the car park and, more importantly, the prison exit; this gave me something to look at and fantasise about walking through. They were mostly singles with the exception of the cell at each end of the row, which was where we were heading. But it was a step closer to getting a single and at least now we would be able to receive all the TV channels, including babe station. This wasn't a lot of use as I never managed to stay awake after 10.30 pm and the babe station babes never appeared on the screen before midnight, or so I was told.

In all honesty, having Chris four feet above me and snoring like the 3.15 from Kings Cross, would dampen my mood for adult TV anyway.

After eating for nearly a week in the VT kitchen, the food on the wing seemed even less appetising, so I skipped the greasy brunch and settled for cereal in the comfort of our new room. The morning's highlight was a couple of games of poker that were accompanied by the constant whining of Bibs about his sentence and ex-girlfriend.

Sunday 7th December 2014

I was beginning to get really annoyed with the constant reminders of Christmas on the TV. Every other advert was for Christmas food, booze or gifts; it was the last thing that anyone serving time in prison wanted to be reminded of. Before getting sentenced I had asked my solicitor if there was any way that he could delay things until January, as I really didn't want to be spending Christmas behind bars. He informed me that one way or another, I would be spending at least one Christmas locked up, so why not get it out of the way sooner rather than later? At the time I agreed with his logic, but as they say, hindsight is a wonderful thing and knowing what I know now I would have pushed for the delay as, even with a four-year sentence handed out in January, I still stood a good chance of getting home or at least being in a category D prison for the next Christmas. The longer I spent here the greater became my misgivings about the law and the legal system.

A visit to church then a long afternoon banged up concluded another week.

Monday 8th December 2014

Life on the inside I felt was opposite to life on the outside, in relation to weekdays and weekends anyway. Most people on the outside would work all week and look forward to the weekends, whereas on the inside it was Monday morning that most inmates looked forward to, for the simple reason that Monday through Friday were busy and therefore the time went a lot quicker. I was not alone in my loathing of the weekends, when there was very little to do and we spent more time banged up. I suppose in some respects we were slightly better off in here as generally, from my point of view, I enjoyed five days of my week and loathed only two, whereas for many on the out it would be vice versa. Back in my days as a fraudster, for instance, every day was a Saturday and I loved every day.

This may sound a little odd to anyone who has never experienced prison, but I can understand why some people would constantly be in and out of prison. Doncatraz was pretty much a boys' club without the bar. For those who weren't as fortunate as myself and had very poor home lives, prison was a nice alternative – three meals a days, no bills to pay and your washing done by someone else. The laundry service was carried out once a week when I'd put all my dirty washing in a bag along with a piece of paper stating my name and cell number, before dropping it off in the laundry room that was located in one corner of each wing. Just before bang up on the same day, I would collect a neatly folded pile of clean laundry, all for no charge. The only down side was that I had to do my own ironing, although even this could be taken care of if you were willing to pay someone a small amount of tobacco. Again, I've wandered off track... Back to why some people were happy to spend large chunks of their lives in prison; the wages in Doncatraz were pretty decent. Wages ranged from £3.00–£6.50 per day, so it was possible to earn £45.50 per week. Aside from the 50p per week TV rental, all of that money was for spending. I know a guy on the outside who works full-time and after his bills, mortgage, petrol and other living expenses he is left with just £30 per week for himself. So, from a financial stand point, some prisoners were definitely better off inside than they where on the outside.

With a spring in my step I left for work with the guarantee of a decent lunch and at least one helping of cheesecake. I'd got a song stuck in my head from a TV advert and couldn't help singing the only line of it that I could remember whilst washing the pots: 'Fly me to the moon'. I believe it was the Marks & Spencer advert and I just couldn't shake it. Despite my out of tune singing, Gavin from sweets recognised it and admitted he was having the same problem with the song. No doubt some advertising executive would be very happy with that result.

Gavin from sweets came across as a decent guy and I was surprised when he told me that this Christmas would be his 14th out of the last 20 that he would be spending inside. He was one of those guys who was probably better off on the inside. He was due to be released shortly after Christmas and would be sent to a bail hostel with just £50 in his pocket. This was the amount that the prisons provided to all prisoners upon release. It had to last him until he began to receive benefits, which would take a minimum of two weeks to sort out.

'How can I make £50 last two weeks? I'll have to go back to robbing and end up back in 'ere before Easter.'

Tragically, that was the circle of life for Gavin and many others like him.

Tuesday 9th December 2014

I had really settled into the routine of things now and the days were flying by. Washing-up wasn't really a bad job and it certainly kept me busy. The ongoing stories of Land Rover theft however, were wearing a bit thin, but then by contrast they made the stories from The Black Shagger more welcome. After work, Chris and I would still call in on John to pass an extra half hour or so. Unfortunately, John's class for the second week was still devoid of students.

At tea time, Bibs joined us at our usual table with his new cellmate who had just arrived into prison that morning. Michael was originally from Gambia but had spent the last 30 years in the UK. He spoke perfect English albeit heavily accented, although I had the impression that he didn't always listen to what was being said. While explaining about his conviction, he had apparently told his solicitor that he wanted to plead not guilty, but due to a misunderstanding his solicitor had entered a plea of guilty. Michael was a suspected drug dealer. His flat had been raided and three ounces of cannabis with a street value of £450 had been found along with £75 in cash. Normally drug dealers have scales for weighing out their wares and bags in which to put them, plus substantially more than three ounces of drugs and a large stash of cash. According to Michael he had nothing to suggest that he was any more than a cannabis user, but despite the lack of evidence the police still suspected that he was a dealer. He was charged with dealing and his apparent admission of guilt earned him a three-year prison sentence, the same amount of time Chris had received for his part in the £1.8 million VAT fraud. I must stress that I have only repeated Michael's version of events and that they may be somewhat different to the actual version of events.

We had a good example of prisoner's stories being slightly different to reality when Clive joined us at the table holding a copy of the 'Doncaster Star'.

'Our friend Austin has made the papers,' announced Clive.

As I stated earlier, Austin had informed us that he borrowed a laptop computer from his mate that turned out to be stolen property. The 'Doncaster Star' told a slightly different story. Above a picture of Austin was the following headline:

'Local man caught in police sting.'

According to the paper, due to a string of burglaries in the local area, police had set up a sting operation. One night they had left a laptop computer on the windowsill of a house, with a small table lamp illuminating it. Austin had spotted the laptop sitting there in the window and decided it was too good an opportunity to pass on. He smashed the window and grabbed the laptop in full view of two police officers that were sitting in a parked van armed with video recording equipment. He was bang to rights. The paper also stated that Austin was to be held at HMP Doncaster until he could be deported.

'Hey Austin, you're famous!' shouted Clive to a nearby table were Austin was seated.

'Fuckin' paper is fuckin' racist; day got all da fuckin' facts fuckin' wrong.'

Please keep that example in mind as you read the rest of this prison diary. While I would never call one of my fellow inmates a liar, it is worth keeping in mind that nine times out of ten I only get to hear one side of the story, the prisoner's side and – most people in here, me included – aren't in prison for being honest people.

Wednesday 10th December 2014

Two weeks until Christmas and I was really looking forward to the season being finished. I had now accepted the fact that I wouldn't be going anywhere yet. It appeared that the 28-day rule didn't actually apply to Doncatraz. The 28-day rule was that a prisoner should be categorised and then moved to a prison of that category within the first 28 days of his sentence. Doncatraz was a category B prison and even if I didn't qualify for D cat, I certainly should not be here.

From what I had picked up from other prisoners, inmates couldn't be moved to another prison until they had received their OASys – 'Offender Assessment System'. This should be carried out within the first 14 days of imprisonment, although according to staff there was currently an eight-week backlog. The OASys was a meeting with a caseworker who would work out a sentence plan with the prisoner. A sentence plan laid out courses that a prisoner needed to attend in order to successfully integrate back into society. For example; prisoners with a sentence for violence may have to attend an anger management course or anyone convicted of a drug-related offence would have to complete a drug rehabilitation course and so on. It was also my understanding that the OASys meeting would finally confirm my category. I was wrong; a prisoner's category is allocated within 72 hours of entering the prison although that does not mean you are automatically made aware of your category. As I mentioned, my categorising officer stated that I 'should be a D category prisoner' and 'I would be notified in due course'. Whether this was to be or not, I didn't know. As it turned out I was not notified of the categorisation decision until much later.

If you are unfortunate enough to be facing a prison sentence, remember that you should be categorised within 72 hours and if, as in my case your category is not confirmed at the first meeting within that specified 72 hours, then submit a general app requesting confirmation of your category. No prisoner should be kept in a higher category than his allocation for any longer than necessary. So, at least, once you know how you have been categorised you can begin to ask questions regarding a transfer to the correct category prison.

After finishing the shift in the kitchen, Steve informed us that there was to be a refurbishment of the kitchen and therefore it would be closed for the first two weeks after Christmas. Luckily we would be serving soup for the staff, so at least our days would be filled and we'd still get paid.

Thursday 11th December 2014

So far I haven't mentioned the many drug addicts who reside here at Doncatraz. When I say drug addicts I'm not talking about the Spice smokers, I mean the hard stuff – heroin. At the cost of millions of pounds to the government all heroin addicts that find themselves in prison are put onto a methadone program. This more or less mirrors the methadone program that takes place on the outside, when the addicts hang around in local chemists waiting for their hit of methadone.

In prison, or at least here in Doncatraz, methadone is issued twice daily, in the morning and again in the afternoon.

My most recent room was located on the top landing so, after my morning shower, this area was a great place to stand and observe the various goings on around the wing. Most of the addicts would walk around the outside of the wing, completing constant but very slow laps in a zombie-like state. At around 8.45 am a PCO on the wing would shout:

'Medication!'

There would be an immediate change; the zombies would suddenly come to life, their sluggish movements would vanish, as they'd virtually sprint across the wing to receive their morning methadone fix. The amount of methadone issued was not enough to get the addicts high but was just about sufficient to stop the sickness and shaking caused from heroin withdrawal.

As a rule, the addicts kept themselves to themselves. They were generally regarded as pretty low forms of life that were only a rung or two above a sex offender.

In the VT kitchen there were a couple of functioning addicts who, in all honesty, didn't seem like bad guys. In fact it was quite interesting to speak with them. I sat with the two guys in question at lunchtime and it soon became clear that they were each at opposite ends of the drug addict scale – for obvious reasons I won't use their names. The older of the two guys was in his late 30s and had been addicted for 20 years and who was desperate to get clean. He knew that this would be an impossible goal on the outside, so he was using his prison time to achieve it. Each fortnight he would request that his methadone dosage be reduced so eventually he could stop taking it altogether and become completely clean. I was slightly taken aback by this; surely the prison should be reducing dosage automatically in order to reduce the number of drugs getting released onto our streets. But this wasn't the case. According to this guy, a prisoner had to want to get clean and had to make a formal request for his methadone to be reduced. This chap was now down to the lowest possible dosage and within the next two weeks he would have his first opportunity to function without it.

The second guy was also a functioning addict but on the outside he was a London plumber and was earning around £2000 per week. At the weekends he would spend all of his wages on heroin. He was serving time for dealing heroin to support his habit and fully intended to return to dealing and taking heroin as soon as he was released. He had just been turned down for a transfer to a category D prison because he had not signed up to a course relating to drug rehabilitation that was specified in his OASys meeting. He now accepted that he needed to complete the course and was due to begin in January; therefore, he would be leaving the VT kitchen. The older guy would also be leaving in January, hopefully to begin a drug-free life on the outside.

Steve had told us that no staff would be replaced until after the kitchen refit, as he was convinced that the two-week timescale that the contractors had given was rather optimistic and would not be met. I believe his words were:

'There's more chance of you getting transferred to cat D than the kitchen getting completed within two weeks.' Cheers, Steve.

Friday 12th December 2014

It was finally Dan's big day, tag day. At some point during the morning after 17 long months in Doncatraz, Dan would be a free man. It was always good to see someone getting his or her freedom. As well as feeling pleased for the man in question it also gave a sense of hope and realization that eventually we all get to go free.

As I had no gym gear, Dan gave me a brand new pair of trainers that he'd purchased for the gym and then never got around to using, along with a couple of pairs of tracksuit bottoms. I now didn't have any excuses for not going to the gym. I knew that working in the VT kitchen was bad for my waistline; I was eating far too well and still managing to consume at least two desserts each day. Once Christmas was over I would start the gym with earnest.

As Dan was packing up his belongings, other prisoners hung around his cell door like vultures. The second he walked out they would be in there, grabbing whatever Dan had left behind – the extra pillows, toilet rolls, tea packs, kettle and TV would all go within seconds. It was a spectacular thing to witness.

As Doncatraz was ultimately a remand and holding prison there was a constant turnover of prisoners, although when *I* would became part of that turnover was anyone's guess. Dan wasn't the only guy to taste freedom. One of the other lads from the VT kitchen had also been given the good news that he would be getting his tag the following Tuesday.

Fridays were generally a lot quieter in the kitchen for some reason. The weekly dose of fish and chips wasn't quite enough to have the staff queuing around the block.

John was still sat alone in his IT class – two whole weeks without students, so Chris and I called in to kill an hour. John was normally good for a story or two and today was no exception. I'll give a little background information before I repeat John's story. As well as methadone there is a heroin substitute called Subutex. Subbies, as they are known in prison, are a blocking agent that is taken in tablet form and are supposed to ease the craving from either heroin or methadone. Again, they are issued twice daily at the same time as the methadone. If a Subutex is crushed up and snorted as opposed to swallowed, as it should be taken, it can provide a high for the person snorting it. The Subutex is supposed to be swallowed in the presence of a nurse but many addicts are able to regurgitate the tablet shortly after taking it and then sell it onto other prisoners so they can subsequently buy tobacco, spice or other drugs. A Subutex tablet is 8 mg and could be split into four pieces; each 2 mg piece could be exchanged for half an ounce of tobacco costing just under £5, therefore, one subbie was worth roughly £20. With that in mind, here is John's Friday afternoon story:

'Did I ever tell you about that mate of mine on security? It was his job to monitor the calls made from the phones in prisoner's cells. As you know, all the calls get recorded; a few get picked at random and listened to. So, one boring Friday night my mate tunes into one particular phone call and hears some woman talking dirty to a prisoner. He decides to stay on the line to continue listening. The prisoner, from what my mate could gather, was masturbating while the woman talked. After a few minutes the prisoner said:

'Speak next week.'

Instead of the line going dead, a second voice came onto the line and said:

'Alright, Mum, how are you?'

My mate nearly fell off his chair. He pulls up all the past calls to that number and checks them. It turned out the prisoner listening to the dirty talk was issued Subutex and was giving them to his cellmate in exchange for a dirty chat with the guy's mother.'

After we finished laughing John assured us that every word was true.

Saturday 13th December 2014

Where had the week gone? It had flown by again and now I was faced with a long, boring weekend. The morning game of poker was, as always, the highlight and I did make the final today, although the runner up doesn't really count for much in poker. It seemed odd not having Dan sat at the table with us, but he was in a far better place now – home.

The weekend took a darker turn when one of the guys on the wing tried to commit suicide. He cut open his arms and wrist on one side. Thankfully, a PCO discovered him before he bled to death and was rushed off to hospital. When he returned to the prison he would be put on a 24-hour watch to prevent any further attempts to take his own life.

Prisoners were checked periodically throughout the night, normally at two-hour intervals. If a PCO was feeling particularly malicious, instead of simply looking through the observation panel in the cell door, he would shine his torch into the cell and dance it around the walls. This would light up the whole room and only the heaviest of sleepers would not be disturbed. I wasn't quite sure what the nightly checks were meant to achieve, as if I wanted to cause harm to myself or even my cellmate, I would simply wait for the cell check and be safe in the knowledge that I had another two hours before the next check.

Monday 15th December 2014

There were two big topics of conversation on the wing today; the first was the change to the phone top up system, which was to come into effect on the 20th December. As I explained earlier, prisoners have two accounts, private cash and earnings. Up until the 20th, phone credit was taken from the private cash account and a daily limit of £50 was permitted. This seemed to be plenty and everyone was happy until a prisoner who was running his business from inside the prison submitted a general app requesting the daily limit be increased, as £50 per day was insufficient. When the powers that be received the application, their attention was drawn to a flaw in the system that had been there since day one and had so far gone unnoticed. Phone credit should have been taken from the earnings account, so for a prisoner not in work or education the earnings account would be credited £15 per week from private cash, if any was available, therefore the prisoner would only be able to spend £15 per week on phone credit. As from the 20th December, all phone top ups would now come from the earnings account.

The second big topic was the 'new regime'. No one was clear as to exactly what was going to change, only that the changes, whatever they were, would be taking effect as from the 5th January.

Doncatraz had received a less than favourable report from the inspector of prisons, who had visited in April. As a result, a new regime was to be introduced that was designed to improve standards.

Wednesday 17th December 2014

I had my first visit with my solicitor since coming to prison. The purpose of this visit was to discuss my ongoing POCA investigation. POCA stood for Proceeds of Crime Act and was brought into force in 2002 so that the state could take back any monies that a criminal made from a crime.

At my sentence hearing, the judge had issued three dates relating to my POCA. The first date was 22nd December; this was the date when I had to submit what was known as a section 18 statement. In this statement I was required to disclose all of my assets to the prosecution. This included details of bank accounts, shares or bonds held, information on properties relating to the values and mortgages on them, plus safety deposit boxes, cars, jewellery or stashes of cash. The section 18 was issued by the prosecution and would list the assets that they believed I had and I would then agree, amend or add to their list.

In my case, I had to give a list of bank accounts along with balances, a list of properties that I owned in both the UK and in Tenerife, including their values and any outstanding mortgages, together with any other assets that I owned.

In most cases, the prosecution already knew exactly what a person's assets were, but they liked to see if there was a possibility if anything was being undeclared or hidden. Once the prosecution had received my section 18 statement, they would respond with a section 16 response. This was to be provided by the prosecution by the second date issued by the judge and was, in my case, the 6th February 2015. This statement would ask for clarifications of details that I had provided in my section 18 statement or bring attention to any assets that I had not mentioned in my section 18.

I had furnished my solicitor with all the information needed to complete my section 18 statement a week before I had gone to court to receive my sentence. Today's visit was to simply sign the document that he had prepared. The visit was brief; I duly signed the section 18 document and was then informed by my solicitor that the prison would not categorise me as a cat D prisoner until the POCA investigation was over. That small piece of information was in for a serious blow.

The third and final date that the judge had issued was the 29th March 2015. Once the section 18 and 16 statements were completed there would be a brief hearing on the 29th March. At this hearing the total value of my assets would be submitted to the court along with the total value of my crime. The court would then order me to pay the lower of the two values or face extra time in prison. Before I get into my figures, I'll give a simple example:

If the value of the crime was £1 million and the criminal had assets worth £200,000, then the criminal would be required to pay back £200,000 within a set time period or face extra time in prison. In the case of £200,000, the default sentence would be an extra two years, which would be enforced if the £200,000 was not paid within a period of six months. Anything over £250,000 would result in an extra five years and over £1 million an extra ten years – so pretty serious.

Back to my situation and the section 18 that I had submitted, it stated that my total assets were zero, or to be more exact, they were in minus figures to the tune of £100,000. The big question was, would the prosecution accept this? At this point I had no idea. If however, the prosecution did accept that I had no realizable assets, I still wouldn't be out of the woods. Having zero assets would mean there would be no confiscation order and no extra prison, but – and this is a massive but – there still could be a benefit figure. The benefit figure was a serious piece of legislation that could be claimed at any point up until the death of the convict. So again, to give an example, if the value of the crime was £1 million and there was no realizable assets, despite paying no money at the time and receiving no additional prison time, the judge could set a benefit figure of £1 million. That £1 million benefit figure would remain as a debt until such a time it was settled. Therefore, if a person with a benefit figure were to inherit £100,000, the state would automatically take that money and deduct it for the benefit figure. If the person was going on holiday, and this happened to a friend of a guy I spoke to briefly in Doncatraz, and the person had £1000 in cash on their person, the cash could be taken and deducted from the benefit figure. All in all it was a pretty bad deal.

Apparently, a good solicitor should be able to negotiate the benefit figure down to a sensible level, so the question in my mind was 'how good was my solicitor?' So far I was having doubts, but maybe now was his chance to shine. No doubt time would tell. I had a feeling of foreboding as I left the legal visit that day.

Thursday 18th December 2014

Today Mr Land Rover didn't turn up for work in the VT kitchen; the reason given by the PCO on his wing was that he was feeling suicidal and wouldn't come out of his cell. The story from The Black Shagger, who was on the same wing, was a little different. Apparently Mr Land Rover had been getting into debt on the wing and was now worried that if he ventured out of his cell the debt would be repaid in blood – his blood.

Debts were one of the main causes of trouble on the inside. The high interest rate didn't really help matters. The normal rate was 'double bubble', so if a prisoner borrowed half an ounce of tobacco, he was expected to pay back an ounce the following week. If it wasn't paid back it would double again, so debt was rife.

Chris was late getting to work as he had been attending the weekly veterans meeting. When he did arrive for work he seemed a little less cheery than usual. He told us about one of the older guys who was also present at the vets meeting. The older guy was wheelchair-bound and appeared to be harmless enough, however, today he had confessed to be serving time because of his capture under the Operation Yewtree investigation that was set up in the wake of the Jimmy Saville scandal. The old man was very open about what he was and what he had done. For his own safety he was immediately wheeled out of the meeting and told in no uncertain terms that he would not be welcome to attend any future meetings.

As I touched upon earlier, sex offenders were hated by all other prisoners and I also believe that most PCOs wouldn't lose a great deal of sleep if they received the odd beating. The slightly unnerving thing was that the sex offender or vulnerable prisoner wing only housed 94 prisoners, yet there were currently over 200 sex offenders serving time in Doncatraz. That meant that there were over 100 spread over the other nine wings. So, at least ten sex offenders on each wing – of course they would all have cover stories – no one in his right mind would ever admit to being a sex offender.

I think this may be a good time to relay a story told to us one Saturday by a PCO. I'll first try to set the scene. Doncatraz is laid out into three house blocks that house inmates. In addition, there is an education block, admin and visits and the main kitchen. The blocks are linked together via long corridors; in some cases there are corridors that are accessible to prisoners. The ones not accessible are the corridors that are open on one side; they are actually more like a footpath with a roof than a corridor. It is along these covered footpaths that the food is transported, on a trolley from the main kitchen to the wing. So, here goes the story as told by the PCO:

'It was one Friday and a phone call came in from 3A, the nonce wing. They were short-staffed and wanted someone from our wing to go to the kitchen and fetch the food trolley. The other two weren't keen to set foot on that wing full of dirty bastards so I ended up going. I wasn't best pleased and was pushing the trolley at a fair rate of knots. Anyway, those walkways make council pavements look to be in good order and the trolley hit a bit of a pothole. A tray of chilli con carne jumps off the trolley and splatters all over the floor. I wasn't going to go back to the kitchen and replace it, so I dashed to the store cupboard and found a rusty old fire shovel. I scooped up all the chilli and a good part of the walkway and slopped it back into the tray and carried on to 3A.' A wonderful story and one I just hope is true.

Friday 19th December 2014

Another week nearly over and there is still no news on my categorisation or my OASys date. When we returned from the VT kitchen there was some good news, however. Emma informed us that there were two single cells available and that one was ready immediately and the other would be available in the morning.

I took the first one, room 315, and Chris agreed to move the next morning. What a great result. The single rooms were the same size as the doubles but felt a lot bigger. Instead of bunk beds there was a single bed with the desk only having shelves on one side, taking up less space. It did feel a little odd after spending six weeks locked in a room with another person to then be suddenly locked in a room on your own. The major plus point was that I would now have a chance to spend more time writing.

Just after tea time bang up, my cell door swung open and the PCO announced that he'd be carrying out a search of my cell, or a 'pad spin' as it was known. Pad spins were very common in the run up to Christmas, as many prisoners made hooch in preparation for the festive period. After a quick look round that lasted no more than ten seconds, the PCO promptly vacated my room empty-handed and re-locked the door behind him.

Saturday 20th December 2014

Saturday morning I received a visit from my parents and partner. Much as prison was not a bad experience, and many of the people I was in daily contact with were somewhat decent sorts, it was pretty special to see people who were not in any way connected to the prison – normal law-abiding people whom you loved. The hour-and-a-half visit seemed to be over before it began though.

This may sound odd, but seeing the people that you love can, in ways, make things that little bit harder. Although it's great to see them it reminds you how much you miss them. Watching my partner walk away from the visits table, knowing I had to stay where I was was one of the most difficult things that I had to endure during my time in prison.

I had to wonder if my partner and also my parents actually believed how decent life was in prison. Did they really think that I was sugar-coating things for their benefit? To a certain degree I would play some things down a little, but generally prison life was every bit as satisfactory as I said it was.

The words of my mate who had served time in the past came flooding back to me:

'It's not really *you* doing the sentence; it's your missus and those close to you on the outside.'

His words couldn't have being closer to the truth. My partner was on the outside living in a small town, full of small-minded people who thrived on other people's falls from grace. She was dealing with gossip and speculation, trying to pay the bills and survive, whereas I was in prison having a pretty reasonable time with good food, plenty of rest, books galore, a wealth of writing time and all with a bunch of interesting people who I would never have got to meet on the outside. I know I've said this before but I'll reiterate – the longer I spent in prison the more I believed that 'prison was a boys' club without the bar.'

Sunday 21st December 2014

News was spreading around the wing about our former wing rep who had attempted suicide a week or so earlier. He had apparently made another attempt on his own life and was in a coma at Doncaster hospital. The rumour was, and again this is only a rumour, that he had been put on suicide watch for two days before returning to a normal cell where he would have had heaps of opportunity and privacy to attempt suicide again. To keep a prisoner on suicide watch was a costly exercise – they have to be literally constantly watched for 24 hours a day. Obviously, someone had wrongly decided his 48-hour suicide watch was quite sufficient for this poor guy.

Wednesday 24th December 2014

Wednesday was the last day in the kitchen before the two-week refurbishment closure. After today we would be having a long four-day weekend and I wasn't looking forward to it in the slightest. A two-day weekend was bad enough, but four days was unthinkable. This would also be my last adequate food for a while. Steve had informed us that once the refit started we would be serving soup and rolls each day in the corridor outside the kitchen.

As I was clearing the tables off during service, I got chatting to a PCO who was part of the security search team. He told me that throughout the search on Friday evening, 167 litres of hooch had been found and confiscated.

Thursday 25th December 2014

Christmas Day was a very sorry affair. That's probably why I haven't felt generous enough to name this diary entry 'Christmas Day'. The highlight, however, was the morning church service, although at the beginning we received the sad news that the suicidal guy from our wing had died in hospital that morning. I cannot think of anything worse for a family than to receive the news of a death on Christmas Day.

After church we were locked up again until the time came for our wonderful Christmas dinner that would be served at 4.00 pm.

Room 315, my new single cell, was located at the top of the stairs on the first floor landing. This location was a double-edged sword. There were two flights of stairs that came up to the top landing and the choice of staircase made by the PCO would determine when my door was unlocked. The staircase that terminated outside my room was closest to the PCO table, so most of the time my door would be unlocked first, but if the PCO had come in through the fire exit after returning from a cigarette break then they would choose the second staircase resulting in my door getting unlocked last. Unfortunately, that was how it panned out on Christmas Day.

I was one of the last five people in the queue for my Christmas dinner. I had noticed that the ten people in front of me had all returned to their tables without gravy on their plates. To say I wasn't happy was an understatement somewhat. I fully accept the fact that this is prison, but can it really be so difficult to make sure that for just one day a year everyone receives gravy? If you asked 1000 prisoners which they would prefer, the chance to vote or some gravy with their Christmas dinner, I'm pretty sure most would go for the gravy. Gravy on a Christmas dinner seemed such a simple thing to expect, yet seemingly impossible for the prison to achieve. Without gravy the taste or lack of taste of the sliced, processed turkey was even more apparent. I'm not proud of what I did after sitting down, but I picked up the turkey slice and threw it at the table – childish, I know. The slice bounced off the table and hit the floor. What sort of turkey slice bounces? I must admit I felt a little better after my outburst, or maybe it was the knowledge of the box of mints and chocolate log in my room that cheered me up.

Monday 29th December 2014

The past four days had dragged and dragged; I'd barely left my room alternating my time between reading, writing, watching TV and of course, drinking tea. It felt good to be heading back to work, albeit only for three days before another painful four-day weekend for the New Year.

Steve was waiting by the kitchen door as we all arrived for work, well, five of us anyway. One lad had been released just before Christmas, another had moved to a different job and Land Rover Man was now considered a security risk. As Bernie explained it in her usual blunt manner:

'We can't have a suicidal man working anywhere near sharp kitchen knives; I don't want anyone cutting himself up on my shift.'

Steve explained that he would only need two people each day and the five of us could work on a rota system. One of the guys asked if we would get paid if we were not on the rota:

'Of course you are; it's not your fault the kitchen's closed.'

After a quick chat amongst us Chris and I decided to work every day while the other three were more than happy to stay on their wings and get paid for the privilege. I couldn't quite understand why they would choose to remain locked up in their wings, but ultimately everyone was happy.

The soup was already prepared and Steve insisted we taste it. In my opinion it lacked flavour.

'Well, give it some flavour then, Jamie fucking Oliver,' growled Steve, trying his best to sound grumpy.

I added a couple of spices including a good portion of pepper and offered Steve a taste.

'That's fucking disgusting – far too much pepper. No one likes that much pepper,' came the expected response from Steve.

All we had to do was serve the soup and collect the money. Well, not money exactly but cardboard tokens. The staff members were required to buy the tokens from the finance department and use them to buy their meals. I suppose it didn't really make sense to have prisoners handling cash.

So far, my kitchen experience had only extended to washing dishes; dealing with 'customers' was quite a novelty. I wasn't joking when I mentioned earlier that we would be serving soup in the corridor. We had a bay Marie on wheels in which to keep the soup warm, a trolley for the take-away containers, bread rolls, butter and a table for the till.

Chris manned the till and I served the soup; today's offering was mushroom soup. Steve allowed us to have as much of it as we wanted during service.

I'd already consumed three cupfuls before our first customer showed up.

'What's the soup?'

'Locally sourced field mushroom, picked by my own fair hand on my way into work this morning.' I felt compelled to dress up the description slightly as 'mushroom soup' sounded so boring.

'Aren't you a prisoner?'

'Yes, six weeks now.'

'Then, how do you get to pick the mushrooms?'

'Steve lets me out for an hour in the morning.'

I could tell by the look on the woman's face that she was trying to weigh up if I was telling the truth or not. She turned to Steve to try and get some sort of confirmation; he shrugged and in a very serious tone said:

'I only let him out for an hour.'

I handed her a container full of hot, steaming, field mushroom soup.

'Would you care to season that before I put the lid on?' Spotting more confusion I pointed to the salt and pepper.

'I'll just give it a quick taste first,' she replied and then after a small slurp, added:

'Just a touch more pepper, I think.'

I had to grin at Steve who mouthed 'fuck you'.

During the hour-and-a-half our soup kitchen was open, we only served ten portions of soup. Now the bar was set I had to come up with an inventive description of the soup on a daily basis.

That afternoon I had another visit with my partner Amy and a friend of many years. As always the hour-and-a-half visit passed far too quickly. I suppose I should be grateful that I got an hour-and-a-half. In some prisons only one hour is permitted.

Tuesday 30th December 2014

After serving Italian tomato soup, made from a recipe that had been passed down from an Italian ancestor of my grandmother's side of the family, Chris had a visit from a Catch 22 worker and was taken away for his OASys meeting.

As we both came to Doncatraz at the same I was pretty confident that my OASys meeting should take place the following day.

I was back on the wing when Chris returned from the OASys assessment not looking too happy.

'They gave me a category C status due to a community service session I missed a few years back. But she did say that when I'm reassessed again in May I'd get a category D then.'

My heart sunk. If Chris wasn't getting a D cat it seemed unlikely that I'd be getting one.

'The assessor I saw when I first came in recommended me for a category D but the manager wouldn't sign it off. It'll soon be May though.'

Chris appeared to accept in fate of being a C category prisoner, but I decided that if I *was* anything but a category D prisoner I would be appealing that decision.

Wednesday 31st December 2014

New Year's Eve. In a few hours 2014 would be gone for good. I, for one, would be glad to see the back of it. At least I knew that at some point in 2015 I would be back at home, at least my UK home. Returning to home in Tenerife was at least another two years away. I was really hoping that today would be my OASys assessment. After serving the daily soup of 'fresh country carrot' and not receiving a visit from Catch 22, I returned to the wing dejected.

Over tea, which again I did not partake in due to the fact that, firstly, I was full with country carrot soup and secondly, it looked simply inedible. A guy wandered over to our table and simply began talking to no one in particular. He proceeded to recite a story about borrowing some burn from someone on his last wing. When the burn dealer returned the next week to collect his half-ounce plus the half-ounce in interest, the guy who had borrowed the burn had smeared his hands with his own faeces. The dealer refused to take the ounce of packet of tobacco from the guy's shit-covered hands and the debt was written off. The guy repeated this exercise many times on lots of different wings. He also had a habit of flinging his own faeces at anyone he didn't like the look of. At this point I was doubly glad I'd chosen not to eat that afternoon.

New year's Eve TV was pretty dire. I was lying on my bed thinking that during the last 38 years of my life, this was the first time I'd ever spent New Year's Eve without company – how tragic. Fortunately I was asleep before the fireworks started erupting at midnight.

Monday 5th January 2015

The year 2015 was here at last; just over two months since I first came inside. The New Year weekend had been as long and as boring as the Christmas one. Today was the beginning of the new regime. On the Friday we were issued with booklets that set out the timetable for the new regime. Below is a copy; I thought it might be interesting for you to see how a typical prison day is set out.

HMP & YOI DONCASTER

FOR PRISONERS

0645 hrs Unlock for early discharges

0800 hrs Unlock for breakfast, medication (basics breakfast in cell)

0845 hrs Lock up. Preparation for activity, works and visits

0900 hrs Visits, gym and off wing work. (other prisoners in cell)

0900—1145 hrs Wing cleaning (wing cleaners only)

1145 hrs Return from off wing activity. Lunch (Basics lunch in cell)

12.30 hrs Lock up

1315 hrs Visits, gym and off wing work. Muslim service Fridays only (other prisoners in cell) except wing cleaners.

1330 –1400 hrs Basic regime exercise

1400—1430 hrs Basic regime—cell cleaning, showers, use of ATM

1445-1545 hrs Exercise

1600 hrs Return from visits, gym off wing work

1600 hrs Gym session for full time workers only

1600 hrs Library session (Tuesdays only)

1700 hrs Lock up

1715 hrs Unlock. Tea, association (Basics tea in cell)

1800 hrs Lock up. Canteen issued Tuesdays only

It was another day serving soup in the corridor and yet another day without my OASys. After a shower and returning to my room to do a bit of writing, Emma popped her head around the door:

'I've got a proposition for you.'

A hundred thoughts passed through my mind.

'I'm all ears.'

'How would you like to work in the library every day after you've finished in the kitchen? They can't pay you but it will mean you're out of your cell all day and it may lead to other things.'

I was sold; the £15 per week that I was earning in the kitchen was more than enough to cover my phone calls and biscuit requirements, so extra money was not a requirement. The major thing for me was the fact that, once I left the wing at 9.00 am I would not be returning until 5.00 pm. Nearly all the other jobs required you to return to the wing at 11.30 am until 1.30 pm for lunch and bang up. But as I already worked in the VT kitchen and had to serve the staff until 1.00 am before eating our own lunch, I would be in the kitchen until around 2.00 pm, and then I would be able to work in the library until 5.00 pm. It could not get much better.

As luck would have it for Chris, there was also a Catch 22 worker on our wing who was due to be released on Wednesday and was going to put in a good word for Chris taking over his job on a part-time basis.

Tuesday 6th January 2015

Once finished with the soup service at 1.30 pm, I headed to the library to start work there. Clive worked in the library along with another guy who was 18 months into a 27-year sentence for drug importation. I had to wonder how anyone could possibly come to terms with a 27-year sentence.

The library had only just reopened after being relocated to a central location within the amenities or education block. Before the move, each house block would have its own small library, whereas now everything was in one central location – this seemed to make a lot more sense. The idea of spreading the prison's book collection over four locations seemed a very odd thing to do.

Now all the books were in one central location they all had to be labelled with stickers stating whether it was factual or fictional. This was my job; a little monotonous but it kept me off the wing.

Back on the wing, Bibs was getting very excited about his up and coming release on Thursday.

'I'm off Facebook for good now and I'm going to keep away from that bitch,' he proclaimed.

In the case of Bibs, everyone was extra happy that he was getting out. He was a decent bloke, but one more story of his ex-girlfriend and Facebook and I'd have to either kill him or myself.

Austin had got a new cellmate, an Asian guy who'd been sentenced to four years for his part in organising sham marriages. As per usual, the guy was completely innocent of any involvement in the scam. His story was that he had simply been asked to attend the service as a favour to a friend; he believed he was merely there to make up the numbers. Police raided the wedding and he, as an apparent guest, was charged with being an organiser. He and Austin unfortunately didn't get along. In Austin's words:

'Dem fuckin' screws only put 'im in my fuckin' cell cause day're fuckin' racists!'

When I was sharing a cell I was lucky enough for it to be with my mate so I can't imagine what it must be like to share a cell with someone you don't get along. But these two took it to a whole new level. As Austin was in the cell first he kept hold of the remote control for the TV, dictating what they should watch and when they should watch it. Meanwhile, Mr Wedding Guest had managed to get hold of a second remote control as their tastes in TV programmes was vastly different. When Austin turned to the programme he wished to watch Mr Wedding Guest would immediately flick the channel over to *his* preferred programme. This would go back and forth all night and end up in a huge shouting match. The two were finally separated after an altercation that I will explain in the words of Austin:

'Dat crazy fuckin' Asian tried to kill me last night. The fucker is a fuckin' racist! I'm on da top bunk asleep and the mad fuckin' Asian jumps on top of me and puts a fuckin' pillow on my fuckin' 'ead. The fuckin' racist was trying to kill me!'

I realize the whole thing is pretty serious but I had to laugh when I imagined them both sat with their own remotes continually flicking channels, then Mr Wedding Guest trying to smother Austin as he accuses him of racism. Only in prison.

Friday 9th January 2015

The kitchen was supposed to be opening on Monday but the work was a long way from being finished. The opening date had now been moved to a week on Monday. Every day while on soup service I'd mentioned to Steve my desire to work on the sweets section when the kitchen reopened. His stock reply would be:

'Well, you aren't going near anything that requires pepper.'

Later in the day while working in the library I had quite a result. One of the managers came in and the librarian happened to mention that I was working there on a voluntary basis. The manager wasn't a great fan of voluntary work and declared that I should be paid. So, from then on I was to receive £3.00 per day for the kitchen and then an additional £1.75 per day from the library. The library job also paid seven days a week so I would now be on the princely sum of £27.25 per week. Not a bad wage by prison standards. Under the new regime a prisoner was only permitted to work one job at a time but, fortunately for me, the VT kitchen was classed as education and therefore a job was permitted. I could see the principle behind the one-job system but the reality was slightly different.

There were roughly 180 positions within the prison and 1130 prisoners, but still many of them remained unfilled. There were two reasons for this; the first was the security clearance system, which at best was farcical. Every prisoner should be cleared for work within two weeks of coming into the prison yet six to eight weeks was closer to reality. Sometimes it could take a lot longer and on more than the odd occasion, a prisoner's clearance could be overlooked altogether and he'd never get the chance to work. The second reason was that many of the prisoners simply did not *want* to work. They had never worked on the outside, so why bother working on the inside? The new regime was meant to get every prisoner into either work or education. The law states that all convicted prisoners should attend work. In my opinion, this created other issues. I'll use the example of the VT kitchen: There should be ten prisoners working there and it's the type of employment where everyone is required to work as part of a team. If two or even one prisoner doesn't want to be there because he's being made to work, it can drag down the rest of the team or ultimately breed bad feeling and possibly violence. I will mention specific examples later on.

It seemed quiet over tea without the ramblings of Bibs, so I think now will be a good time to introduce Johnny Gold Teeth. Johnny was on remand for his part in a big drugs conspiracy and if nothing else, he certainly looked the part. He reminded me of an English version of Goldfinger's henchman, Oddjob, from the Bond film *Goldfinger*. The only difference was that, from the neck down, every visible inch of Johnny's skin was covered in tattoos. The other thing likening him to a Bond villain was his teeth – every single one was gold. I couldn't help but imagine what the twelve members of a jury would think while looking at Johnny standing in the dock: shaved head, tattoos peeping out from above the collar of his expensive suit and to top it all, a set of gold teeth. I know justice should be blind but I'm sure if the Oxford Dictionary contained pictures then next to the word 'drug lord' would be a picture of Johnny. From what Johnny told me about his jewellery, which of course he couldn't wear in prison, he'd make Mr T look like a rank amateur. Although Johnny looked mean and spoke in a deep and very gravelly voice, he was an extremely laid back man and would help anyone out without looking for personal gain, which was very unusual in prison.

Saturday 10th January 2015

The weekend came and went without incident; however, two brothers from Romania joined the poker game on Saturday morning. They were both serving a short sentence for burglary. It was quite interesting speaking to the brothers about the differences between English and Romanian justice. They thought that prison here in England was some sort of joke; apparently many Romanian hotels didn't come close to the standard of accommodation offered here at Doncatraz. They were even impressed with the food. I couldn't possibly agree with them on that point. At the moment I was only eating cereal in the morning and then soup at lunchtime at work. In my experience, prison food was very heavy and stodgy. Maybe there was more thinking behind this than we realized. I am only speculating here but I suspected that, after a heavy meal, the first thing you would want to do is sleep and not run around the wing causing trouble, or maybe it was just down to cost. The one thing I had learnt from working in the VT kitchen was that all the food was bought in from a single outside supplier. This particular supplier provided food for the armed forces, schools and hospitals as well as prisons. The food was also graded; for example, grade one would be the best. When I say 'best' I mean the best the company offered. Grade four or prison grade was the lowest grade. All the food that arrived into the prison was clearly stamped with 'prison consumption only'. In the past the food for the VT kitchen, which is where the staff eat, was purchased at the local market, but in times of costing, this practise had been cut and now the food for the VT kitchen came from the same source as the rest of the prison food. Prisoners in Doncatraz were fed three meals for the bargain price of £1.87 per person per day.

Monday 12th January 2015

There was still no news on my OASys assessment or categorisation decision. I had decided to wait until the end of the week then on Monday I would submit a 'COMP 1' complaint form. It didn't make any sense to me that Chris, who came into Doncatraz at the same as me, had been given his OASys assessment and I hadn't.

Work consisted of serving soup again. By this stage, I was getting a little bit fed up of eating soup every day but, on balance, it was still far better that eating the food on the wing and at least I wasn't putting on any more weight. Today's soup was oxtail and, as always, I felt it necessary to dress up the description of it. Today it was 'Kobe oxtail' as in Kobe beef. I gave all my customers the full spiel: 'Kobe oxtail, flown in from Japan this week, where for the past six months the aforementioned ox had its tail massaged on a twice-daily basis with a belly rub by two Japanese virgins.'

Thankfully, we only had twelve customers so I didn't have to repeat myself too many times.

After finishing the duties of the soup kitchen, it was off to the library. The prison librarian, a very stern lady who seemed to dislike everything about her job, informed me that there was a job coming up in the new prison magazine. Always up for a challenge I headed off to meet the lady who would be running the magazine. After a chat I agreed to join the magazine as a staff writer. There were still some administrative issues to overcome before the magazine could go into full publication, so it was agreed that I would be notified in 'due course' when my services would be required. That little phrase unnerved me a little but the woman in charge seemed very assertive, so perhaps her 'due course' wasn't the same as everyone else's in the prison.

I was fast coming to the conclusion that there were lots of things on offer in the prison, if of course you wanted to embrace them. It was quite possible to fill more or less every waking hour.

Over tea, Johnny Gold Teeth was very pleased with himself; he'd managed to get himself a job on the servery. Security wouldn't clear him for an off-wing job for some reason or another so he was restricted to working on the wing, which meant either wing cleaner or servery and all of those positions were quite hard to come by.

Tuesday 13th January 2015

Tuesday wasn't much better than any other day apart from a guy on the top landing who suffered a Spice attack. As I came back onto the wing after work, two medical staff were rushing to assist another Spice attack victim. Each week there was an average of ten cases where medical staff had to attend. As I mentioned before, Spice is used for relaxing carp when they're being transported. When smoked it has a similar affect to smoking cannabis, due to the fact that it slows the heart down, thus causing the sensation of relaxation. However, as stated earlier on, if too much is smoked the heart can slow to such a degree that the smoker passes out or, in severe cases, the heart stops altogether. Spice attacks can take many different forms depending on the quantity smoked or the strength of the Spice. Spice, as with most other drugs, is usually 'cut' with other substances to increase the dealer's profits. I had heard one instance where a particularly inventive prisoner had grilled some broccoli until it charred, then crumbled it up and sold it as Spice. Over the course of my time in Doncatraz I witnessed various different types of Spice attacks, which I will detail later.

Monday 19th January 2015

As always, my Monday morning routine consisted of checking the ATM. To my delight after checking the timetable it stated the glorious word: 'OASys' – 10.30 am. At long last, after eleven weeks of incarceration I should be getting some clue as to when I may be moved out of Doncatraz and to a better place.

My original caseworker, Dave, had for some reason been replaced by a lady called Amanda. I was sitting in the unused classroom that was used for storing the trolley for the soup kitchen, with Steve and Bernie from the kitchen. Chris was also in attendance when Amanda entered the room.

'D cat prison, here I come,' were my first words to Amanda as a way of greeting.

'You're not going to D cat,' chimed in Steve.

'He's right, you're not,' stated Amanda.

My heart sank; she's got to be kidding or winding me up. Chris and Bernie left the room to set up the soup kitchen while Steve remained seated at the table where Amanda sat me down to begin my OASys. Before she could open the file, I asked:

'You *are* joking aren't you, about me not going to D cat?'

She flicked through the file and stopped when she came to the ICA1 form, the one that had been completed on my first morning a lifetime ago.

'There – category C – the countersigning officer didn't approve your cat D recommendation,' she replied, pointing to the open page.

I stared in disbelief at the sheet. There was a box with the heading 'Reason for refusal of category'. The reason for refusal was 'unknown confiscation order'. To me it was obvious why the confiscation was unknown, there wasn't one. I glanced at the date on the sheet – 7/11/14. The decision had been made over two months ago and I hadn't been notified. I could feel the anger rising up inside but somehow I managed to keep myself in check. The OASys meeting was important and would follow me throughout the remainder my sentence. I told myself to be cool and try to say all the right things.

'If you're not happy, you *do* have the right to appeal,' said Amanda, as if sensing my displeasure.

'I think it's safe to say that I'll be appealing,' I replied, trying my best to remain pleasant.

Category discussions were now clearly over and it was time to begin the OASys or Offender Assessment System. Before I go into detail on this, I think this is a good opportunity to emphasise a couple of facts for anyone who may be facing prison or even for those already inside. For anyone else, well you never know; remember - justice is blind. Firstly, a prisoner must be categorised within the first 72 hours of coming to prison. Secondly, if after your categorisation meeting you are still unsure of your category because 'it needs to be signed off by a manager', do *not* wait to be 'notified in due course'. Submit a general app requesting notification of your category. Thirdly, and I feel most importantly on this – just because you have been given a category doesn't mean it's correct. You have the right to appeal.

Back to the OASys, to be honest, I felt a bit like I was present at my own school parents' evening. The first thing Amanda recited to me was my wing report. This was written by the PCOs from the wing and went as follows: 'Craig is a polite and compliant prisoner and abides by the prison regime without exception'. I felt a little embarrassed for some reason; although it didn't help having Steve sat a couple of feet away. Next it was time to talk about my crime.

'Your file is a bit vague, so I did an Internet search and even that didn't give me much information. But as I understand it, you stole £1.3 mil–' began Amanda.

I couldn't help myself and had to cut her off with, '£1.8 million.'

'Excuse me?'

'We stole £1.8 million, not £1.3.'

'Oh okay, so you stole £1.8 million from the taxman?

'Sorry, no, it was the VAT man,' I corrected.

I could see that Steve was pretending to read something but I knew he was listening.

'Okay, Craig, tell me in your own words about the crime,' prompted Amanda.

So, I did. I watched her face as I told the whole story, all the time wondering if she was going to ask the question. I wasn't disappointed.

'So, have you still got any of this money stashed away?' she asked at the end of my monologue. Then she seemed to think better of it.

'I shouldn't have asked that, so don't answer it.'

Next we moved onto the awkward part.

'Tell me why you decided to embark on this crime.'

To say I was just a greedy individual probably wasn't the right answer, so I told the truth about a period of financial hardship that led me to stray from the path of honesty.

'And how do you feel about the victims of your crime?'

Now that *was* an interesting question. The VAT man was the victim and the VAT man was responsible for sending me to prison for four years. He was then going to try and recover the money that I'd worked so hard to steal. Did I feel bad for the VAT man? No, not really. Maybe I'm just looking at things from a convicted man's point of view; maybe it wasn't really the VAT man that I was stealing from but the public. Was that money destined for schools, hospitals or all the poor unemployed people? Was I denying some bloke on the sick, who hadn't worked a day in his life a new car? Maybe I'd even denied an MP a second duck pond - who could say? My silence seemed to say it all.

'Okay, Craig, I can understand that perhaps you don't view the VAT man as a victim, but how about all those people whose identifications you stole?'

Another bad question or good question depending on which side of the table you were sat. The truth was, yes, I'd stolen people's identities and obtained VAT numbers in their names, but I hadn't used those identities to run credit and bad debts, therefore the people in question were completely unaffected. Were they really victims? I realized that I was over-thinking things. Trying to sound as genuine as I could, I replied:

'I feel really bad about those people. It must be awful to know that there are criminals out there who can steal your identity and do what they like with it. They must feel so violated. I'd never really given it any thought before.'

I could have continued but Amanda smiled and scribbled some notes on my file.

There is a wide range of courses that prisoners have to complete in order to become rehabilitated. For example, drug users have to complete a course on the evils of drugs; the wife beaters and violent offenders attend an anger management course and nearly all prisoners are recommended to complete a course known as A to Z. The A to Z course deals with motivation or how to overcome the lack of it, although Amanda pointed out that anyone who was already in prison employment was not deemed to have a motivation issue. As I was currently doing two jobs, don't have an issue with drugs and have no violent tendencies, Amanda was finding it difficult to find a course that suited my needs.

'I'll put you down for victim awareness; you probably won't qualify but I have to put you forward for at least one course,' she stated, after reviewing all my data. I had to wonder for whose benefit the courses were for; the prisoners or the prison that would be receiving the funding for the course.

Amanda concluded by explaining that all my data would be fed into a computer to generate an 'OASys score'. The OASys score was the likelihood of I offending in the future and would be displayed as a percentage. Chris had scored 52%, which according to the computer meant he was quite likely to reoffend. If I could beat that score I'd be happy, as prison hadn't yet dampened my competitive side. Amanda was of the opinion that my score would be in single figures. All I had to do now was carry on doing exactly what I was doing and I would leave prison a reformed man. What wonderful news, the system really must work. To be fair to Amanda, she had been a really good sport and, although I was very unhappy about my category, I knew it wasn't her fault.

Once we set up the soup kitchen I told Chris the news. I think to a degree he was pleased that we were still in the same boat, both C category prisoners. The only difference was that Chris had taken his C category on the chin and was happy to wait until May for his re-categorisation, whereas I was not. As soon as I got to the library I intended to begin my appeal. When Steve joined us at the serving table his first words were:

'My God, you can spout some shite.'

'I don't know what you are talking about, Steve,' was my reply, feigning offence.

'All that shite about feeling sorry for those poor sods whose IDs you nicked.'

'It's all a game, Steve.'

'And you play it so well. Speaking of shite, what are you going to call my minestrone soup today?'

When I got to the library I relayed the story of my OASys and categorisation to Clive and, as luck would have it, to another prisoner. The latter I shall refer to as 'the unofficial solicitor'. He was serving an 11-year sentence for PPI fraud and had so far battled his confiscation from £29 million down to £3.8 million and was still fighting. After hearing my account and asking a few questions about my background, he offered to write my appeal for me and do the same for Chris. The unofficial solicitor had already dealt with appeals on behalf of seven other prisoners, of which six had been successful.

'The first thing you need to do is fill out a general app, request a copy of your ICA1 form and any documents that support the denial of your category D status,' the unofficial solicitor instructed.

I didn't need telling twice. The unofficial solicitor also told me that if I were so inclined it would be a good idea to read the PSI on categorisation. I had no idea what a PSI was, but soon learnt that it stands for Prison Service Instruction, which is a document issued by the Ministry of Justice that lays on the rules and regulations that a prison must adhere to. There is a PSI for every aspect of prison life, from what should be contained in a prisoner's breakfast pack to how to deal with a prison riot. PSI documents are available in all prison libraries. If, as is sometimes the case, the staff are resistant to giving out PSI documents, ask someone on the outside to download the document and post it in. The difficult part is to know which PSI to ask for. The PSI form relevant to my case was 'PSI 40/2011 - Categorisation and re-categorisation of adult male prisoners'. (Make a note of that if you have an up-and-coming court appearance). A PSI is also a wonderful thing to quote from; a staggering amount of prison officers, prison management and even solicitors are not wholly familiar with the information contained within PSI documents. I located the PSI in the library and read it with great interest, making notes as I read. I was now feeling very confident about the appeal of my C category allocation.

Towards the end of each working day, the manager would pop his head into the library to ask if there were any problems. Today he pulled me to one side and asked if I was any good on computers.

'I've forged over 5000 documents from petrol receipts to passports.'

'In that case, you should be more than qualified. Would you like a job in the computer section of the print shop in the afternoons?'

I'd more or less finished adding labels to the books in the library so agreed to start work in the print shop the following afternoon. The shop closed at 4.00 so I was still able to spend the last hour in the library. Happy days.

Tuesday 20th January 2015

First thing that morning Chris and I filled out general applications requesting a copy of our ICA1 forms and, in my case, the information that supposedly supported the presence of a confiscation order. Once the form was completed I made a phone call to my solicitor, which after the usual pleasantries, went something like this:

'John, can you confirm that at present I don't have a confiscation order in place?'

'No, you don't, but you do have an ongoing POCA investigation which may lead to a confiscation order. Why do you ask?'

'My category D has been turned down due to the fact I have an outstanding confiscation order, so could you confirm what you've been told in writing, please?'

'I can put it in writing but it won't make any difference; you can't go to a category D prison while there is an ongoing POCA investigation.'

I suspected that my solicitor wasn't familiar with PSI 40/2011, but I wasn't going to argue.

'Just send me the letter and I'll deal with the rest from in here.'

'Okay, it'll be in the post tonight.'

Should I be worried? This was the second piece of incorrect information that I'd received from my solicitor. Actually, I will correct that – this was the second piece of incorrect information as far as I was aware. I had read the PSI cover-to-cover and nowhere did it mention that persons under a POCA investigation could not be sent to a category D prison.

As soon as we were let off the wing, Chris and I headed straight to the door of Catch 22 where Amanda's office was located. Amanda answered the door:

'You two are going to be a thorn in my side, aren't you?' she smiled.

'Oh-h yes,' I replied, trying to sound like the dog from the Churchill advert.

We handed her the general apps and she promised to give them priority.

Steve informed us that this was the last week of serving soup in the corridor and the kitchen would reopen on Monday. Great news, decent food again; I was getting a little tired of soup every day. After finishing the soup service and having lunch of yet more soup, I headed to the print shop for my first afternoon's work. Keith, the manager of the print shop as well as the library, let me in through the heavy metal gate and gave me the customary pat down. He then led me to an area containing several computers and a vast array of printers. It was a forger's paradise; good job I was well on my way to becoming a reformed character. Keith pointed me to a computer and handed me a stack of photographs.

'Scan these, clean up the image, enlarge them to A4 and print them out on glossy photo paper.'

With that, he was gone. Talk about getting thrown in at the deep end. I stared at the computer screen – Photoshop was the logical choice. I was quite pleased, as I've always wanted to try Photoshop but never had the chance – the joys of prison. After a bit of messing around I got the hang of it and managed to carry out Keith's request. It was most enjoyable and the time flew by. At 4.00 it was back to the library for the last hour.

When I returned to the wing everyone had been locked away.

'What's going on?' I asked the PCO who let me onto the wing.

'There's been some fun and games this afternoon. Someone cut the cord off his kettle and then used it as a weapon to beat another guy around the head with. The plug made a real mess of his head.'

I was told later that the guy who carried out the attack was paid a 'Spice joint' to administer the beating that easily could have resulted in loss of life. It is amazing the lengths some people will go to in order to have something that is worth less than a pound on the outside.

Thursday 22nd January 2015

I spent the morning back in the kitchen cleaning, ready for Monday's opening. We were down to four staff, one of whom would be getting released on Monday, so come opening day there would only be three of us and, of those three, Chris and I had so far only washed pots.

During the cleaning session, Amanda entered the kitchen carrying a brown envelope. She handed it to me, saying:

'Here you go. Hopefully this will keep you happy and off my back.'

'You know I won't be happy until I'm on a bus to a category D prison.'

She nodded and left. I ripped open the envelope and was disappointed to find only a copy of my ICA1 form but no supporting documents. I was hoping to see a letter or e-mail stating that I had a confiscation order in place, although deep down I knew that this could not be possible as there *was* no confiscation order in place. Regardless, I'd be back to Amanda first thing in the morning to ask for the supporting documents. The PSI states that under the 2002 Data Protection Act, a prisoner is entitled to view all information held about him. I'd enjoy quoting that in the morning.

After finishing in the kitchen I went to the print shop for the afternoon. I asked Keith for some work and he assured me that he'd bring some over shortly. Maybe he should have said 'in due course', as the work failed to materialize. Instead, I spent the afternoon playing around with Photoshop and chatting to a guy who had recently come onto wing 1B. I'd not spoken to him before but had heard a few rumours. Apparently, he was a gun nut and when the police raided his home they had found enough weapons, ammunition and explosives to start a small war. Wing gossip isn't always the best way to learn about people so I decided to just let him tell it his way. For once, the wing gossip was actually less sensational than the truth. I wouldn't class the guy as a gun nut but more as a gun and weapons enthusiast or perhaps fanatic would be a more accurate description. The guy had an arsenal of weapons ranging from automatic machine guns to Glock handguns. The extent of his knowledge regarding weapons was amazing. He also had a gift for re-commissioning weapons; in fact, he viewed it as a challenge to reactivate a weapon that had been de-commissioned. He told me he'd read on the Internet that it was impossible to re-commission a Glock pistol. To this guy, reading that was like a personal affront to his abilities. After reading the article he immediately purchased a de-commissioned Glock pistol, which is perfectly legal to do, and set about the supposedly impossible task of re-commissioning it. He told me that, after a bit of research and purchase of materials from America, he achieved the impossible and re-commissioned the gun. When the police firearms specialists found and tested the weapon, they refused to concede that it was once a de-commissioned weapon. A Home Office department, which specialized in weapons, also stated that it was impossible to re-commission a Glock pistol. That was until they examined the weapon and saw the guy's handiwork. The guy went on to tell me that the Home Office was currently in discussions with his solicitor regarding a deal on his conviction. If the guy was willing to work with the Home Office technicians and show them how he re-commissioned the weapon, he could get a reduced sentence. At the moment, his solicitor had advised him to expect somewhere between five and 20 years. I considered this to be a vague estimate on his solicitor's part, but I held my counsel. All in all, chatting to this guy made an otherwise boring afternoon quite interesting. To emphasize the point I made earlier, prison certainly gave one an opportunity to meet some very interesting people whom one would never normally come into contact with on the outside.

Walking back into the library for my final hour, Clive greeted me with:

'You're a man in demand today.'

Apparently, the lady who ran the prison magazine had been looking for me to start work with her. Typical that I'd now started in the print shop. I went in search of her and told her that I'd speak to Keith who'd hopefully release me from the print shop to work on the magazine. Under prison rules, if a prisoner quits a job he is not permitted to apply for another for one month, but a prisoner can change jobs with his manager's consent.

For me once again, tea time was a high point of the day and not because of the food. It was a chance to sit down, relax and have a laugh and a joke with some of the decent guys on the wing. Not actually eating tea was a huge plus also in my eyes. There was no need to stand in a queue that seemed to be getting less orderly by the day. Then there was the added bonus of not having to consume the slop that was passed off as 'food'. So, from roughly 5.00 until bang up at 6.00 each night, it was downtime. There was always plenty of banter and story exchanging around the table. There was one guy in particular, who would join us for tea intermittently. He was on a short sentence for growing cannabis and for some reason he always ended up with strange cellmates. He'd only been inside for two months and was already on his fourth cellmate. This wasn't a reflection on him as a bad cellmate but his rather laid-back manner. He never objected when a PCO would ask if he would mind sharing with a new guy coming onto the wing. The latest man to be thrust upon him was serving a short sentence for harassing his own wife but seemed to have a fear of going anywhere near the showers. Cannabis Man was having a good moan about him:

'He fucking stinks. I've tried dropping hints like opening the windows and spraying deodorant around. I've even offered to lend him some shower gel, but he turned me down.'

We were all laughing, but on a level you had to feel sorry for Cannabis Man. Once the banter had subsided, Clive suggested that it might be a good idea to speak to one of the PCOs. In any other circumstances, speaking to a PCO about another prisoner would be seen as 'grassing' and was the ultimate sin in prison, but as with every rule there are exceptions and this was one of them. Despite giving us a laugh it wasn't much fun being in such a small space with someone who didn't shower. Cannabis Man obviously liked the idea, as no sooner had Clive finished his sentence when he was on his feet marching toward the PCO table. A couple of minutes later he was marching back across the wing towards his cell with a PCO in tow. The PCO, who will remain nameless, stuck his head into the cell. Cannabis Man told us later what the PCO had ordered:

'It fucking stinks in here. If you don't get your arse into the showers within the next two minutes I'll be back with a bucket of cold water!'

It did the trick as, a minute later, a guy who looked like he'd been sleeping rough for a month emerged from the cell and trudged toward the shower block. Cannabis Man looked very relieved.

Friday 23rd January 2015

As soon as I got off the wing, I headed straight for the Catch 22 office to speak to Amanda about my missing information. I was informed by one of her co-workers that she didn't work on Fridays, so I'd have to wait until Monday. Monday felt like a lifetime away, but there was nothing more I could do except wait. One virtue that I was learning here in prison was patience. Nothing moved fast; it was something that serving prisoners had to accept.

We spent the morning carrying out the final kitchen clean before Monday's opening. After carrying out my last soup kitchen duties I had soup for lunch – hopefully for the last time. Once I arrived at the print shop for the afternoon session, I spoke to Keith about changing the shift from print shop to magazine.

'We're far too busy to let you go; I've already lost one computer operator to them. You could always write for the magazine in your own time,' was Keith's response.

So, that was that. I was staying in the print shop where I spent another afternoon waiting for work to appear 'in due course'. I did, however, receive a master class in making explosives from household cleaning materials from the gun fanatic. I very much doubted that I'd ever need such information, so although he didn't get my full attention, it did pass the time.

You could guarantee the library was always a good place for stories and gossip. The supervisor who covered Thursdays and Fridays normally had a good story or two to share. When I arrived at the library, a conversation was already underway regarding undercover police officers that were sent into prisons to gather intelligence. I had always thought it to be one of those prison myths, but our library supervisor, who was employed directly by the prison, confirmed it to be true. In fact, there had been one such undercover officer planted in the prison a couple of years before. The library had been his point of contact. One day he had walked into the library and handed a piece of paper that had a phone number printed on it, to the supervisor, and told her to call it immediately. Apparently, his cover had been blown. Thirty minutes later he was escorted from the library and never seen again. Maybe he was just a deluded prisoner and is now sitting in a padded cell somewhere. I wasn't too sure how useful prison information could be, as most people tended to either greatly exaggerate or seriously play down their crimes, not forgetting that a lot of the serving prisoners were 'innocent' anyway.

Saturday 29th January 2015

I mentioned earlier how fast gossip or information can spread around the wing. Well, on Saturday morning during association, some bright spark decided to tell another bright spark that the reason for Cannabis Man's cellmate not wanting to shower, was because he was a paedophile and was worried for his safety should he venture into the shower block. Within two minutes everyone on the wing thought the shower dodger *was* a paedophile. A group had gathered outside his cell door and were banging on it. Luckily for the shower dodger, Cannabis Man had read his court papers and confirmed to the growing mob that he wasn't a paedophile, just an old drunk who enjoyed harassing his ex-wife. Now in the mood for confrontation, the mob turned on to the bright spark that had started the untrue rumour. Thankfully, the mob of 15–20 had raised the attention of the two PCOs, who had now left their coffees and were stood close by. The rumour starter was immediately dragged away and escorted to another wing for his own safety. Why someone would invent something like that, which could have fatal consequences, was beyond comprehension.

After making it to another poker final before suffering a run of bad hands, it was back to the room for a bit of reading - thirty minutes' to be exact before the door swung open for lunch. The new regime gave us a lot more time out of our rooms at the weekends, although to be honest, once lunch was out of the way I was happy to stay in and either read or write until 3.00 when it was time to go to work in the library. Saturday was wing 3A's library day. 3A was the wing where the sex offenders were kept so they had to have library time when no other prisoners where present. No prisoner from 3A could move around the prison without being accompanied by an officer. This was for the safety of the prisoner. As I have mentioned twice, sex offenders are universally hated throughout the prison. 3A was officially called the VP, which stood for vulnerable prisoner wing as it was meant to house any prisoner that was considered not suitable for general population. However, as the majority of sex offenders were not housed in general population, most prisoners assumed that anyone housed on 3A was a sex offender.

I realize that this may sound wrong but I found myself looking at each and every one and wondered if they were indeed a sex offender or some filthy paedophile. Some I felt just had a look about them that made me feel uncomfortable just breathing the same air as them. I was sure that even on the outside, if I saw some of them stood outside a school gate, I'd feel exactly the same. After finishing the library shift on a Saturday, I was always very keen to get back to the wing and straight into the showers. I always felt dirty merely being in the presence of some of the 3A prisoners.

Monday 26th January 2015

Of course, my first point of call Monday morning was Amanda.

'Will I ever be shut of you?' was her greeting.

'Afraid not. I seem to be missing some information that I requested.'

'The powers that be have said that you cannot see the e-mail regarding confiscation. You'll just have to take their word for it.'

'But according to PSI 40/2011, page 8, paragraph 1, I can see all the information that you hold.' I hoped that I'd quoted the right information, but was confident that it would not be checked, so on balance it didn't matter.

'There are some names on the e-mail that are considered sensitive and I'm sure that not having the e-mail will not affect your decision to appeal, will it?'

She was right, of course, but I was not comfortable with being asked to take someone's word on something that I knew to be incorrect. No point arguing so I thanked her and left for the kitchen. Decent food again, I couldn't wait. I was also looking forward to having a free rein of the sweets section.

'Mr Lowndes, I'm afraid you're being thrown in at the deep end, but I'm sure you'll cope,' announced Bernie as I entered the kitchen.

There was a new guy on pots, but that still only left four of us doing what ten men would normally do.

After my first day working in the kitchen making dessert, I was bitten by the bug. I loved it and, with the exception of setting fire to my first attempt at carrot cake, the day had been pretty successful. Once the sweets were made I got a chance to work on the servery, dishing out the food to the staff. It was a nice change from serving soup and was defiantly better than washing pots. Again, I stuck to the theme of dressing up the description of the dishes and really laid on the friendliness. I would always kick off with a friendly:

'Good morning/afternoon, sir,' followed by, 'What delightful dish can I offer you today?'

It was obvious that it caught one or two of the staff off balance, although that said, 99% would respond in an equally friendly manner. The one thing that did surprise me was the amount of bitching over the price of the food compared to the portion sizes. A main meal was £2 and a dessert £1 - an absolute bargain in my humble opinion. Once service was over and the last of the diners had left we could eat our own lunch, which was defiantly the highlight of the day for me. Over a splendid lunch of steak pie, potatoes, carrots, peas and gravy followed by fresh cream scones and a delicious chocolate wellington, the four of us lifted our cups of water (a glass of wine would have made the lunch perfect but alas, you can't have all) and we made a toast to Doncatraz.

It was odd looking round the dining-room; there was no indication at all that we were in prison. After lunch and a final clean-up, I left the kitchen at around 2.00 pm to start work in the print shop. When I say 'start work', what I really mean is: turn up and attempt to amuse myself for a couple of hours.

Friday 30th January 2015

The week had flown by. I think it was my best week so far since coming to prison. I'd enjoyed every minute of it. Working in the kitchen was a defining thing that was making my time so enjoyable. On my way to work I called in to see the lady who ran the prison magazine. She agreed for me to write articles in my own time and type them up for submission once I'd finished 'work' in the print shop.

When I arrived back on the wing later that afternoon my spirits were lifted further; awaiting me was a letter from my solicitor. It confirmed that I currently did not have an outstanding confiscation order but was subject to an ongoing POCA investigation. At last, something positive from the solicitor. This was exactly what I wanted to hear. Now I had all the information necessary for the appeal against my categorisation. So, Monday afternoon I would give all the information to the 'unofficial prison solicitor' and let him work his magic.

There was still 15 minutes left before bang up and Chris popped into my cell and told me a story from the veterans meeting he attended. I'll share that story with you now.

When we first came onto wing 1B nearly ten weeks ago, a guy introduced himself and explained that he was an expert with TV aerials. In fairness to the guy, he made an aerial for our TV that enabled us to receive over 100 Freeview TV and radio channels, so no arguments with his ability there. The guy whom I will call 'Aerial Man' told me he was so good with aerials because he used to be a radio operator in the army. Each week he would head off to the veterans meeting with Chris and join other ex-soldiers who were currently serving time. The idea of the veterans meeting was for ex-service personnel to get together, share stories and generally give one another support. With each passing week, Aerial Man's stories, from when he served time in Afghanistan, would get more exaggerated. He would tell stories of opening fire on groups of Afghanistan civilian men or carrying out unspeakable acts of violence against women and children. I'm sure that there may be the occasional case when a rogue solider breached the rules of engagement, but this guy seemed to have done it on a daily basis. Chris had asked him on a couple of occasions what his army number was and each time he was unable to remember it. As any serving, or ex-service person will tell you, a service number is something that you never forget. After a bit more pushing, he finally remembered it and recited it to Chris. Chris was a little concerned, however, as the service number that Aerial Man had quoted fell into a group that would have been issued 30 years ago. This would have meant that Aerial Man had joined the army aged six. The organisers of the veterans meetings had also picked up on this fact.

Unfortunately for Aerial Man, it had become recent practice to check out the service numbers of all ex-forces personnel who attended the veterans meeting. When the checks came back on Aerials Man's service number it turned out that it was not a genuine one. The group organiser pulled him to one side and informed him that he had been rumbled and was no longer welcome at the meetings. Aerial Man's explanation was a little different and went something like this:

'I've got a bit pissed off with those veterans meetings; all those stories about people seeing their mates getting killed is depressing. I don't think I'll be going again.'

No one on the wing was completely sure what Aerial Man was in prison for. His story seemed to change every time he told it. I'm not saying that he had something to hide. Maybe he just had a disorder of some kind; after all, pretending to be ex-forces was a bit more than the everyday lies you heard. I actually knew a guy on the outside who had a similar disorder, although a severe case of it. He was incapable of telling the truth about anything. If he told you he'd eaten toast for breakfast, chances were that he'd had cornflakes. The tragic thing about Aerial Man and this guy was that they actually believed their own lies. As I'll speak more about the man on the outside later on, I'd better name him. I think Jack-an-ory is quite apt. The older readers will remember *Jackanory* from kids' TV; I think the name came from rhyming slang for story.

Monday 2nd February 2015

Monday was my favourite day of the week. It felt good knowing there were five busy days ahead. It did feel strange to know that I was now entering my fourth month of imprisonment. Where had the past three months gone?

After another busy morning in the kitchen and an equally quiet afternoon in the print shop, I headed off to the library. I hoped the unofficial prison solicitor would be there, as I had all my paperwork with me relating to my categorisation. Luckily for me he was there and, after a quick look over my papers, declared:

'You should definitely be a category D prisoner. There is no reason whatsoever why you should be categorised as C.'

He went on to instruct me to get photocopies of my paperwork, then he would write my appeal and submit it the following Monday. It wasn't long before Chris appeared in the library and was given the same news. The unofficial solicitor informed us that our appeals were going to be part of a package of ten appeals that were all going to be submitted as well as getting passed to IMB. IMB is the Independent Monitoring Board and is there to ensure that prisoners are treated fairly by the prison. IMB have a post box on every wing, which is normally next to the post box for applications that I mentioned earlier. If a prisoner has any concerns about his treatment within the prison, he can submit a form to IMB that would be looked at and dealt with by a person who is independent of the prison service. In many cases, the people from IMB were volunteers with a passion for ensuring that prisoners were treated fairly. Obviously I was not alone in wondering why so many prisoners were getting C categorisation when they should clearly be D category. I also had to wonder how many prisoners had simply accepted their categorisation or knew nothing about the appeal process. Chris was an example of this. As I explained earlier, he had accepted that he was a C category prisoner and was happy to wait until his next assessment in May when he may or may not get re-categorised. I know I've said this before but I believe it is important enough to keep repeating. Just because you are told something verbally or even in writing by an inmate, an officer, a manager or even a governor does not mean it is correct. Do your own research; ask someone on the outside to research it for you and if in any doubt, appeal. While I'm on the subject of advice, I'll share something else that I've learnt here in Doncatraz. If you have any outstanding debts when you come to prison, for example, an outstanding balance on your credit card, an overdraft or personal loan, these can be written off. This, of course, will depend on the length of your sentence and the financial establishment you owe money to. If you are only serving a few weeks then you will probably not qualify. But anyone sentenced to 12 months or more, will. All you need to do is get someone on the outside to contact your bank or credit card company and explain where you are. Quite often your prison number and prison address will be required. The bank or credit card company will send you a form at the prison to sign. Simply sign the form, send it back and that will be the last you hear of your debt. The other positive to this is that your credit rating will not be affected. The debt is simply shown as settled on your credit file. It is also worth contacting your local council, as serving prisoners are not liable for council tax on their homes.

Friday 6th February 2015

The week had flown by again as usual. Another guy had joined our dinner table. It was odd how people seemed to just melt in and out of the foreground. One day they weren't there, the next they were chatting like you had known each other for years. The new guy, whom I'll call 'The Fall Guy', was serving a four-year sentence for fraud. The fraud involved the buying and selling of land and, from what I could gather, The Fall Guy hadn't benefited from the fraud. In fact, it was quite the opposite. He'd lost everything. It sounded as if his business partners had set him up, taken the money and left him to face prosecution. In his summing up, the judge had even stated that he didn't believe that The Fall Guy's business partners existed. It was his defence barrister who had advised against calling the ex-business partner to the stand. The Fall Guy was possibly too nice and laid back for his own good, but he was good for a wind-up and always took it in good spirits.

'Lowndes!' shouted one of the PCOs. I walked over to the PCO table to see a large, brown envelope. The PCO handed the letter to me unopened, which meant it was a solicitor's letter. All other post is opened in front of the prisoner and a percentage of incoming and outgoing post is opened by security, checked and then resealed. All solicitors' letters are labelled 'Rule 39', which means the contents are confidential and are not to be opened by anyone except the prisoner. In Doncatraz, this rule was well adhered to; however, this is not the case in all prisons. It is, of course, presumed by the prison that a solicitor wouldn't be silly enough to send cash or any other contraband in a letter, although I have heard rumours to the contrary. The envelope was A4 and the thickness of a pack of playing cards. I ripped it open as I walked back to our table. The document contained within was a section 16. A section 16 is a response document to the section 18 that I submitted in December. It detailed the prosecution response to my statement of assets and asked for various clarifications. The original figure that the prosecution were alleging was £1.378 million. In my section 18 statement, I'd put forward a case showing my assets to be worth roughly zero. The section 16 prosecution response had now moved to £283,000, so in my eyes, they were getting closer but still had a way to go to come round to my way of thinking. I now had to prepare a section 17 that was a response to the section 16 – hope you're following all this. The section 17 should provide evidence that I *didn't* have the £283,000 that the prosecution were now alleging. The most interesting and, to a certain degree, worrying part of the section 16, was something called hidden assets. The hidden assets figure was €200,000 (euros). This was the figure that the prosecution could prove had been withdrawn from ATMs in Tenerife while I was living there. The interesting part is that in my basis of plea, which the prosecution accepted, I stated that a third party took half of the money that was withdrawn in Tenerife. But that fact was obviously not important any more. I will attempt to explain the prosecution's thinking when it comes to hidden assets. Over a period of time I allegedly took the whole €200,000 and didn't spend a cent of it. Instead I hid it all away in a box somewhere, therefore, it is still available for me to go and collect and hand over to them. I thought this sounded very unrealistic, but unless I had receipts to prove where the €200,000 had been spent; the prosecution would assume I still had it stashed somewhere. When times were good I would think nothing of spending €300 or €400 on a single meal, but would I ask for a receipt? Sadly not. Luckily, I had an ace up my sleeve to deal with – hidden assets – which I'll talk about later. I imagined that most people who were faced with the problem of hidden assets would have no way to prove where the money had been spent. So, it came as no surprise to learn that only 3% of confiscation orders are ever satisfied. I was really hoping that I would become a member of the 3% club by handing over a nominal £1. The only trouble with this was that it was in the hands of my solicitor, so time would tell.

The good thing about Fridays was that there was always a friendly PCO on duty, so Chris and I managed to get all our documents photocopied ready for submitting our appeals on Monday. We made four copies in all; one for Catch 22 who were responsible for the categorisation process and appeals, a copy for the unofficial prison solicitor, one for ourselves and finally a copy for IBM who were now showing more than a casual interest as to why so many prisoners were appealing categorisations.

Monday 9th February 2015

After a pretty uneventful weekend it was time to submit my categorisation appeal. There was a separate post box on each wing that was solely for complaints and was emptied each morning. All complaints, which my appeal was classed as, had to be responded to within five working days. So, all being well I would hear something by next Monday. I wasn't overly confident judging by how slowly most other things were dealt with in here.

The weekend had yielded one useful thing, however. Each week since coming to prison I'd been sending letters and buying my own stamps. I had now established that the prison pay postage on two letters each week so there is no need to have any more stamps sent in – a good thing to know for the rest of my sentence. Pity it took me so long to find out.

Wednesday 11th February 2015

Wednesday morning was usually an interesting time as it was debt repayment day. As I mentioned earlier, canteen is delivered after bang up on a Tuesday evening, so Wednesday is the time when the debts from the previous week are called in. For anyone who has borrowed burn or bought Spice on credit, it is payment time. The washman was responsible for visiting various cells and collecting debts. It was fascinating to watch him moving from cell to cell then leaving a minute or two later with items from biscuits to tobacco. I never saw him with a pen or paper so he obviously had a good memory for figures and faces.

As usual, my morning in the kitchen consisted of making a selection of hot and cold desserts. Next, I would spend an hour on the servery dishing out lunch to mostly friendly staff. One thing I could not understand, even on the outside, was why on earth anyone would be so rude to someone who was making or serving their food. I've seen it many times in kebab houses. A drunken person will hurl abuse at the guy taking his order and then believe that the man behind the counter is going to disappear into the back of the shop and make the kebab with love. So here I am in prison and I have to wonder why a member of prison staff would be rude to a prisoner making and serving their lunch. After all, prison officers and prisoners are not traditionally the best of friends anyway, so why make matters worse? As I mentioned before, when I was on the servery I would adopt a very friendly and helpful manner. This in itself would throw some of the staff off balance, as I think that some of the staff believed that they were far superior to us lowly criminals. So, to have a lowly con speaking to them in a civilised manner was indeed a shock. To be fair to most of the staff, it was probably a novelty to be spoken to by a prisoner in a polite manner. For the most part, staff would return the friendliness and some would even engage in a little light-hearted banter. There were, however, one or two members of staff who were quite unable to return a simple 'good afternoon' let alone the follow-up question as to how they were. No matter, each day I would persevere, hoping that perhaps once I might receive a nod or even a smile. On this particular day with one of the worst culprits of ignorance who is a great fan of hot puddings, returned to the counter wearing her customary scowl and asked:

'Do you have a comments form?'

From her tone she may as well have added 'you low-life piece of shit'.

I glanced at the empty bowl in hand and wondered if she perhaps wanted to write a positive comment about the quality of her meal. As her tone didn't really confirm this I thought it best to check:

'I'm sorry, madam, what is it you require?'

'A comments form; I wish to record my dissatisfaction at today's hot pudding. It wasn't sweet enough and the custard was disgusting.'

I must admit, the custard *was* like water. For some reason, custard was my nemesis; I just couldn't get it right. It was either lumpy or, like today's effort, watery. I had the feeling that she wanted an argument and was expecting me to defend it. Not a chance.

'I quite agree, madam, that custard is bloody awful. I'm amazed you didn't refuse it when it was served.'

I kept staring at the empty bowl. She had managed to consume every last bite of the pudding and all of the shitty custard before moaning about it.

'Well, it's unacceptable,' she continued.

'This is a training kitchen, madam, and I have only being making desserts for two weeks,' I replied, doing my best to remain calm.

At this point, Bernie, our tutor, appeared behind the complaining woman.

'Well, in that case, your tutors are obviously very poor!' snapped the woman, before walking to the cold dessert display cabinet and helping herself to a slice of cheesecake. She then bypassed the till and returned to her table with a smug look on her face.

Bernie is ex-military and can only be described as tough but fair. She keeps us all in check but one thing she will not tolerate is our efforts in the kitchen getting knocked by a member of the prison staff. She was not happy and I knew that the ignorant complaining customer would be in for a few choice words at some point.

After cleaning up in the kitchen I headed for the print shop for the afternoon session. I'd just sat down at my computer when Keith the manager shouted:

'Okay, gents, that's it for today. Everybody back to your wings!'

I checked the clock; it was only 2.10 pm, which was unusually early to be sent back to the wing. When I entered the wing, it was deserted.

'To your cell, Lowndesy, we're on lock down,' instructed a PCO.

Lock down meant that every prisoner was to be locked in their cell. It could be down to a number of reasons: a missing prisoner, a security issue or a cell search. I just hoped it wouldn't be a long lock down.

At 4.30 pm my cell door opened.

'Pass your plate and bowl out!' barked a PCO.

I had eaten a typically large lunch in the kitchen and, as I never ate on the wing anyway, declined the offer of whatever the PCO was passing off as food. I told him to give it to someone else.

Thursday 12th February 2015

I awoke at my usual time of 6.30 am, still not having left the cell since I was banged up the day before. At 9.30 the door opened and a carton of milk, small pack of cornflakes and a brew pack were kicked through the door.

'Are we getting out today?' I asked the PCO.

'Not a chance, maybe tomorrow if you're lucky.'

My heart sank; it already felt like a lifetime since I'd last been out. About an hour later a notice was pushed under my door. The notice stated the following:

NOTICE TO ALL PRISONERS

Further to the theft of prison property I have had no option but to lock the prison down and carry out a full search.

As a consequence of this there will be no activities today other than:

Legal visits
Domestic visits (Afternoon Session)
Dentist clinic
Optician's clinic

A decision will be made later today regarding the regime tomorrow. You will be notified of this accordingly.

The Director
12 February 2015

I wondered what could have been stolen that would result in the whole prison getting locked down. Working in the kitchen with knives carried a lot of security. If all the knives were not accounted for at the end of each session, no one could leave the kitchen until the missing knife was found. If there were to be a missing knife, the lock down would be isolated to that particular area and wouldn't result in a full lock down, so I had to conclude that this must be something pretty serious.

Around 11.00 am, I could hear activity out on the wing. The observation flap on my door wasn't fully closed and through the gap I could see a few prisoners stood in the shower block on the ground floor. Another hour passed before my door opened and two PCOs stood outside it.

'Cell search, wait downstairs,' said the first PCO.

'Don't make a mess in there,' I said, only half joking.

Some of the staff that carried out cell searches had a reputation for making a serious mess. Everything would be thrown onto the floor, pictures ripped off the walls and letters scattered. I suppose a lot was down to the prisoner's attitude. As I walked down the stairs I firstly noticed that one of the pool tables was piled high with pillows, duvets and mattresses. On another one there were at least ten flatscreen TVs.

The second thing I noticed was the large box-like chair that I had sat on when I first came into the prison. It was the device that scans for anything that may be concealed in a prisoner's anal cavity. A PCO standing next to the chair called me over and instructed me to sit down on the chair scanner. After around 20 seconds the PCO told me to get off the chair and wait in the shower block. There were eight or nine other cons waiting in there when I walked in.

'What are they looking for?' I asked no one in particular.

Three or four guys all started speaking at once. Before I relay the story to you, I must emphasize that it is only what I was told on that day in the shower block, therefore all or part of it may or may not be true. The story went like this:

A prisoner had managed to steal a video camera from the media centre. The media centre was where the prison magazine was produced. It also housed audio and video equipment that was used for a course that was run by the prison education department.

After stealing the video camera, the prisoner had allegedly embarked on a mission to film as many things as he could in the prison. One such section of film consisted of two PCOs giving a prisoner a bit of a kicking. A member of staff had since found the video camera, although it had been smashed into many pieces. The problem for the prison was that the memory card that contained all the footage was not within the camera, so the lock down was to enable the prison staff to search for the missing memory card. Talk about a needle in a haystack. According to the story, the memory card had already been handed out on a visit. If that were the case, it would probably already be on YouTube by now. I had to conclude that the version of events must at least be partly true or the search of the prison would not have happened.

After ten minutes or so the PCO opened the shower block door and told two others and I to go back to our cells. As I got to my door, the two PCOs who conducted the search were coming out.

'Did you find anything?' I asked.

'No, all clear,' was the simple reply.

The place was exactly as I'd left it, so no complaints there. The one thing I did notice was that my second pillow had been taken. Half an hour later a bread roll and a pot of egg mayonnaise was delivered to my door. It was not my normal choice of lunchtime cuisine, but it was either that or to starve. I gratefully accepted it. Apart from the ten minutes that it took to search my cell, I'd been locked away for 24 solid hours. Tea was delivered at around 4.30. I was getting serious cabin fever by this point and only ate the food to break up the monotony.

Friday 13th February 2015

At 8.00 am my cell door opened and stayed open. Forty-two long hours of lock down had finally ended. As I came out of the cell, Jonny Gold Teeth was walking towards me down the landing.

'That was just like the old days, locked up for 23 hours a day, food eaten in the cell and back then we had no TVs. We didn't even have a toilet, just a bucket in the corner that had to be slopped out once a day if we were lucky.'

I had heard that in some prisons meals were still eaten in prisoner's cells. We were pretty lucky here at Doncatraz. The prison was only 20 years old but was well kitted out. Some prisons were still using buckets for toilets up until 2005. It was bad enough having just a curtain between you and your cellmate when using the toilet. I couldn't imagine what it would be like to use a bucket and then not be able to empty it for hours.

When I arrived in the kitchen, Steve informed me that he'd had words with the ignorant complainer from Wednesday. To be honest, I think that Steve just relished the opportunity to have a go at someone. The complainer didn't make an appearance in the kitchen for lunch today. After an uneventful service, I headed to the print shop where a lady who was in charge of the visits café was waiting to see me.

'I'm looking for someone to work in the visits café at the weekends and Steve has put your name forward.'

I agreed to take the job, as working weekends was very appealing. The time should fly by now. As you know, weekends were the one part of the week that dragged for me.

That evening, another guy joined us at the table. Clive knew him from when he first came to Doncaster. He had since been transferred to another prison but, due to a court appearance, was spending a few days back here at Doncatraz. I'm going to refer to this guy as Double O Billy. He was serving a three-year sentence for a scam involving dating websites. Double O Billy had set up a fake profile on a dating site. He would then start chatting to older, professional ladies and claim to be a secret agent who was working deep undercover. So deep, in fact, that he had no access to his main bank account or credit cards. He would then persuade those ladies, there were four in total, to send him money to help out with his day-to-day living costs until his assignment was complete. Only two of the ladies agreed to press charges against him and he was convicted of obtaining £30,000 by deception. Double O Billy did disclose to us the exact figure that he had obtained through the deception, but alas, that will have to remain a secret. The amazing thing was that one of the ladies was still sending him money while he was in prison. The prosecution had argued that Double O Billy had taken advantage of vulnerable women; however, his defence team managed to persuade the judge that the women were merely gullible and not vulnerable. Defrauding vulnerable people is a much more serious offence than defrauding gullible ones. Apparently, the local press had put a picture of Daniel Craig next to a mugshot of Double O Billy and made a few unflattering comparisons. His story generated a lot of laughs around the table. The conversation soon turned to my categorisation appeal and Double O Billy, who appeared to be an expert on categorisation and that, as I was fast learning, there were many experts in prison, told me in no uncertain terms that someone in my position would not be going to a category D prison. He told me that Doncatraz had promised him a category D position and then sent him to a cat C prison instead. The one thing that keeps you sane in prison is to take everything anyone says with an EU salt mountain. Everyone is an expert on everything and if you believed everyone's advice you would go mad. I decided to offer him a bet; just to see how certain he was of his own advice. If he was proved right, my appeal failed and I did not end up getting my D category, I would pay off his £30,000 confiscation order. If, however, he was wrong and I got my D cat, I would expect him to pay me £30,000 towards my confiscation. Despite his earlier self-confidence, he declined the bet. What a surprise.

Saturday 14th February 2015

At 9.30 am, Chris and I headed off to the visits area to begin work. One of the other guys from the kitchen was also starting work that morning. I'll have to give you his name, as I think it's such a great one you don't come across every day – Storm Blueit. I kid you not – what an awesome name. Besides the three of us from the kitchen, there were two other prisoners who worked the café in the week and two female staff members. To say that it was a little crowded in the tiny work area was an understatement. The two staff members began explaining to Chris, Storm and I how the café operated. I noticed that one of the weekday workers had yet to move from his leaning position against the counter. Both his hands were firmly wedged down the front of his jogging bottoms and hadn't moved since he'd been stood there. What a great advert for hygiene.

The visits café menu was pretty basic; just burgers, toast and a selection of hot and cold sandwiches, which included bacon and sausage. Once the first visitors started coming in, it was mayhem. The orders were flowing thick and fast. The weekday guy had managed to pull one hand away from his groin and, with an un-gloved hand, took care of adding beans and cheese to the sandwiches. He was yet to speak or even smile. After just twenty minutes' service, one of the ladies sent him back to his wing. The other weekday worker definitely meant well but was causing chaos. He was finally given his marching orders when a fierce-looking lady of the larger build wearing ridiculously tight leggings came to the counter and ordered a cheeseburger. With another un-gloved hand he picked up a handful of grated cheese and deposited it onto a waiting burger. The lady was not pleased:

'Oi, you dirty fucking bastard! You can fuck off if you think I'm eating that now that you've had your dirty fucking hands on it!' she spat.

Thirty seconds later he was gone. Losing two workers certainly helped matters and we soon fell into a routine and got the orders out quickly and hygienically. The shift flew and by the end of it the staff were pleased with our efforts and asked if the three of us would be happy to work every weekend. We all readily agreed. As well as filling up a normally boring weekend, we were able to eat food that was a vast improvement on what was on offer on the wing and, then of course, there was the money. The visits café paid £6.50 per day; a whopping £13 for the weekend. Considering that five days in the VT kitchen only paid £15, visits was great money. My weekly wage was now a mind-blowing £40.25 per week. The day was split into two shifts: 9.30 am–12.00 pm and 1.15 pm–4 pm, Saturday and Sunday. After completing my first full shift I understood why the pay was so good; we'd earned every penny of the £6.50.

Sunday 15th February 2015

The morning shift was a little quieter than it had been on the Saturday although I was still amazed at the number of beefburgers we managed to sell before midday. Not my first choice for breakfast on a Sunday morning, but each to their own.

The first problem occurred, however, before the start of the afternoon shift. At the weekends the cell doors weren't unlocked until around 1.30 pm. I had told the duty PCO that I had to be at work in the visits café no later than 1.15 pm and therefore needed unlocking at around 1 pm. At 1.10 pm my door was still locked so I pushed the call button that illuminates the red light outside my cell indicating that assistance is required. Officially, the call button is only supposed to be used in an emergency although prisoners would push it for any number of reasons. It was a full twenty minutes before a PCO appeared and unlocked my door.

'I have to eat my lunch,' answered the PCO curtly when I asked why it had taken so long to come to my door. I have no argument with PCOs eating lunch but what I *did* have an issue with was a PCO taking a whole twenty minutes to answer a call. The PCO would have had no idea why I'd switched my light on; I could have been attacked by my cellmate or experienced a medial emergency. But as the PCO pointed out, the call was not an emergency so it was irrelevant that it took so long. I was not going to argue the point so just kept my silence and headed off to the visits café. I finally arrived 30 minutes late. The visits staff were used to prisoners finding it difficult to get PCOs to co-operate so luckily there wasn't an issue. Again, Sunday flew by and another week of my sentence was over.

Monday 16th February 2015

There seemed to be a bit of tension in the kitchen on Monday morning. Two of the lads were moaning that it was unfair that the weekend shifts in the visits café had been given to just the three of us. They voiced their feelings of dissatisfaction to Steve. To keep the peace, he duly drew up a rota, which included all seven of the workers from the VT kitchen. Of those, there were at least three of them whom I knew I would not be able to work with in a cramped and busy environment such as the visits café. Two of those three were the ones who had started complaining about not getting the shifts. To be honest, I didn't like the idea of working in close proximity to these guys so I told one of the moaners that he was welcome to take my weekend shifts. Chris, who was of the same opinion as me, offered his shifts to the second one. The two lads were most pleased with this outcome, although Steve wasn't happy – he now had to redo the weekend rota.

'In my day, when you were given a job you stuck to it and didn't just quit,' he sniped.

I thought it best not to respond but thought that, when you're given a job and carry it out well, you shouldn't have half of it taken from you. Harmony in the kitchen was more important than earning a few extra quid. I was sure that I should be on my way to

D cat in a few weeks' time, so no need to rock the boat.

There was also a bit of drama at the end of the shift when one of the sharp knives was unaccounted for. At the end of every session, Steve had to count and return all the knives to a locked cabinet. After a full search of the kitchen the knife was still missing.

'You'll have to search the bin bags,' announced Steve.

At first I thought he was joking – no such luck. We'd emptied four bin bags before the knife was innocently discovered in a pile of potato peelings.

Back on the wing at tea time there was a noticeable absence at our table. Double O Billy had been sent back to his C cat prison. Lucky man.

Tuesday 17th February 2015

During the morning in the kitchen I received a visit from one of the Catch 22 orderlies to see if I would be available to meet Mr Pete Cooper at 1.30. Pete Cooper was the manager of Catch 22 and had also countersigned my ICA1 form and refused my category D status. I had no idea if he would be the bearer of good or bad news, but at least it was movement so I was grateful for that at least. About half an hour later, Pete Cooper walked into the kitchen and asked for me.

'I was passing by, so thought I'd call in and put you out of your misery,' he begun. He then went on to tell me the news I'd been waiting to hear for the past few months.

'After reviewing your ICA1 form and receiving some additional information, I can now confirm that your categorisation has been changed to D.'

I could have kissed the guy! Even though I knew I should have been a category D prisoner, it felt great to hear it officially.

'You'll be notified in writing within the next day or two,' he added.

I asked him if he had also looked at Chris' appeal; he obviously had as he dismissed me and called Chris over. Pete confirmed that Chris too would be re-categorised as D but there was a slight difference. He had already replied to Chris' appeal and turned it down, but since then he'd had reason to change his mind. He told Chris to ignore the paperwork that was on its way and consider himself a D cat prisoner like me. So it was now official – we were both D category prisoners and both allocated to HMP Sudbury, which was closer to home and a step closer to release. I was on a serious high now. The first thing I did when I got back to the wing was call the missus – voicemail, bugger. I remembered that she was on her way back to Tenerife. I called my dad with the news. I've always been positive about everything in my life, sometimes overly so. My father, on the other hand, was the voice of reality and stated:

'You've still got to get there.'

That was true. Just because I was now officially a D cat prisoner did not mean I would suddenly get transferred to a D category prison. I had to wait until there was transport travelling there, amongst other things. Sudbury was not the local category D prison to Doncatraz, so it could be weeks or even months before I moved. I decided that no matter what, I was not going to wait months.

Wednesday 18th February 2015

First thing, I managed to get hold of the good lady in Tenerife and give her the good news. I just about managed to tell her before the phone suddenly died.

When I returned from work that afternoon, there was a brown envelope pushed under my door by internal post. I ripped open the envelope to see that it was the reply to my comp 1 appeal. In the response section of the form, it read:

'After receiving further information I am happy to review your categorisation'.

The form was signed by Pete Cooper – so far, so good. A couple of minutes later Chris came to my door, who had also received his response. The response was exactly how Pete Cooper said it would be. It was a straight denial of Chris' re-categorisation. As Chris had been told to ignore it he wasn't fazed.

Thursday 19th February 2015

After leaving the kitchen on Thursday, Chris and I bumped into our caseworker, Amanda.

'I'm finally getting rid of you then; bet you're pleased about the re-cat?'

She told us that there were around eight other people who were allocated to Sudbury so it shouldn't be long before transport was arranged to move us.

After another extremely boring afternoon in the print shop I headed to the library. A few of us were discussing my allocation to D cat when Keith the manager came in and asked what we were talking about. I told him about finally getting my D cat status and was wondering how much longer I was likely to be stuck in Doncatraz for.

'Remind me on Monday and I'll make to call to my mate; he's in charge of ship outs and will be able to tell me when you're going.'

This was great news. According to the Internet, and as mentioned before, the first thing a prisoner would know about moving to another prison was a slip of paper under his door the night before. I already knew that I'd find out about my move three or four days in advance as the kitchen would have to be notified of my departure, but an exact date would be perfect.

Another thing that I'd read many times online were words to the following effect:

'You may feel that you have been lost in the system, but you haven't, the system works slowly and you will move through it. You can do nothing to speed it up'.

In my experience this was untrue as with many things in life you can change them with a little effort.

Friday 20th February 2015

After another normal working day, I got back to my room to find another brown envelope waiting for me. Internal mail again. I eagerly ripped it open to find a single sheet of paper marked 'Categorisation and allocation confirmation'. The feeling of joy was overwhelming; it was now official. The sheet of paper had my name, prison number and new category 'D'. I showed Chris the paperwork. He looked it over and noticed something that I hadn't. Next to the words 'prison allocation' was written 'Oakwood' and not 'Sudbury'. Was nothing straightforward? I'd never heard of Oakwood let alone know where it was. I was sure that Clive would know. Over tea, Clive informed me that Oakwood was located somewhere south of Wolverhampton. Wolverhampton was about an hour and twenty minutes away from home, so I didn't really want to end up there. My spirits took a bit of a dip. It did give a bit of ammunition for some banter at the tea table though:

'Oakwood is actually a Cat A prison.'

'Oakwood is where they send all the nonces.'

It was the usual sort of thing and I took it in good spirits. No one had seen Cannabis Man all day so Clive asked a passing PCO where he was. Apparently, he had been shipped out to a category D prison. Cannabis Man had only seven more days to serve on his sentence before getting released on HDC; again, I had to wonder what the point was of moving a prisoner to another prison with only a week left to serve. Once back in my room, I grabbed a general app and filled it out, requesting that my prison allocation be changed from Oakwood to Sudbury.

Monday 23rd February 2015

On my way to the kitchen I stopped by the Catch 22 door. I gave the door a hard knock and, when it was answered, asked to speak with Amanda:

'Do you have an appointment?'

'No, but I'll only need two minutes maximum.'

I was sure that everyone used that line but the lady disappeared down the corridor. A couple of minutes later, Amanda came through the door.

'Will I ever be rid of you?' was her greeting.

'When you get me onto that bus for Sudbury – yes. Speaking of which...' I handed her my allocation confirmation sheet and general app. 'I appear to be going to Oakwood. Could you sort it out for me?'

'Anything for a quiet life; leave it with me.'

She took the papers and returned to her office.

I went to the kitchen eager to find out how the two moaners had got on in the visits café. I was still a little annoyed that Steve had decided to dilute the shifts, but perhaps quitting altogether wasn't the best move. That said, I had actually enjoyed the weekend. I'd won at poker on Saturday morning, pocketing six packs of biscuits in the process and worked in the library in the afternoon. Sunday morning, a visit to the chapel and then the remainder spent writing so, all in all, a good weekend. As I walked into the kitchen, Steve informed me that someone else would be joining me in sweets. One of the lads from pot wash had now been elevated to sweets due to someone new starting in the kitchen. Bernie thought the guy looked like someone off the TV called Bones and the name had stuck. The kitchen was the only place he was known as Bones, so I shall continue to use this name.

Bones was serving time for supplying class B drugs and was still managing to run his drugs supply business from inside the prison via a mobile phone he had managed to acquire. This was not the first time that Bones had spent in prison. He told me that in his last prison he had a PCO on his payroll. I asked him if he had one on his payroll here in Doncatraz but he refused to answer. He did, however, say that he knew of at least one PCO on his wing that was bringing Spice into the prison. Whether this was true or not we will never know.

One of the guys who had been complaining about not getting the work in the visits café had only lasted one hour into his first shift before quitting. The other guy didn't enjoy the work and said he wished he'd kept his mouth shut. Apparently, Sunday had been a disaster with burnt food, complaints from customers and long waiting times. I felt a bit sorry for the two ladies who ran the visits café, but it was out of their hands. Chris had been on a visit on the Sunday and had explained to them why he and I were no longer working there; they completely understood.

I spoke to my dad that evening and he told me about some problems that were occurring due to the efforts of Jack-an-ory; you will remember I mentioned him earlier. A few years ago, Jack-an-ory and I had conducted a couple of business deals and now he was attempting to blackmail me. That was the one thing that really frustrated me about being in prison; people would try to take advantage of the situation. Unfortunately, being locked up meant I had very little control of things on the outside. I knew that Jack-an-ory was below average intelligence, but to try and blackmail and obtain money by deception was especially stupid considering I was under a POCA investigation. Much as his behaviour wound me up, he was a father to a young child so I really didn't want to see him landing himself in prison as well. Sadly, with the way he was behaving, the situation could only have one outcome.

Tuesday 24th February 2015

Amanda visited me at work to hand deliver my amended allocation confirmation. I studied the sheet; the word 'Oakwood' had been crossed out and replaced with 'Sudbury'.

'The girl in the office wrote Oakwood by mistake; it's always been Sudbury in the computer, but I knew you wouldn't have left me alone until you had it in writing,' Amanda explained.

I was pleased at the news but also a little annoyed. It was the little things I found hardest to deal with. When someone is informing a prisoner about his next home for the remainder of his sentence, would it be a big ask for that person to double-check what they wrote? Maybe I was blowing this little mistake out of proportion. The matter had been compounded due to the fact that I'd had the weekend with it playing on my mind. On the other hand, if I was the type of person not to complain I could have spent weeks worrying about it.

Wednesday 25th February 2015

Nothing against my new sidekick, Bones, but I definitely preferred working on my own in the kitchen. We spent a lot of time laughing and joking, but this seemed to take the emphasis off the making of the sweets, which I must confess I had begun to get a serious passion for.

When I got to the print shop, I remembered what Keith had said the week before about finding out the exact details regarding my move to Sudbury. I had a word with him; he took me into the office and dialled his mate who was in charge of transfers.

'It's me, mate, how are you?... Yeah, I'm good. I need a bit of info from you... a prisoner of mine... Mr Lowndes, allocated to Sudbury. Any idea when he might be going?'

Keith nodded a few times, exchanged a bit more small talk and then hung up.

'You'll be going within the next two weeks.'

I couldn't believe it. Two tiny weeks and I'd be in a Category D prison – fantastic!

Friday 27th February 2015

When I returned to the wing that afternoon, everyone was talking about a murder that had taken place on 1A. 1A was located directly below our wing and remember, it was where I had begun my time in Doncatraz. Everything I'm about to relay is only what I was told by other prisoners, so draw your own conclusions.

The murdered guy was a 43-year-old who was serving a short sentence for shoplifting and was due to be released in two weeks' time, however, he had served a previous sentence in the 90s for rape. News of the man's previous conviction had somehow become common knowledge on the wing. A 26-year-old lad who had managed to get into a bit of debt on the wing had been told that if he gave the 'rapist' a beating his debt would be cleared. The 26-year-old was also told that the shoplifter was in fact a sex offender and was using shoplifting as a cover story.

The shoplifter was stood on the top landing leaning over the railing watching a game of pool below when the 26-year-old had approached him and hit him on the side of the head. The shop-lifter had not seen the blow coming and was completely unprepared for it. The shoplifter had fallen and, on his way down, had smashed his head on the metal railing. The shoplifter had died soon after hitting the floor.

Wing 1A was on lock down and the police had been called in to carry out a full investigation. The 26-year-old had been arrested, charged with murder and was due to appear before the Magistrate's Court on Monday morning. There was a rumour that other people were also to be charged with conspiracy to commit murder.

Saturday 28th February 2015

I had a visit in the morning from my parents and partner. It was always good to have a visit but the hour-and-a-half seemed to be over before it had really begun. The visits served to remind me about the one truly bad thing about prison life, being kept away from loved ones.

As expected, my dad was sceptical about me getting moved to Sudbury within the promised two weeks. After all, it was my original belief that I would not be spending any longer than 28 days in the holding prison. Just goes to prove how wrong the Internet can be sometimes.

We discussed Jack-an-ory and decided the best policy was to leave it up to the financial investigators who were dealing with my POCA to sort things out. He had declined his chance to finalise things in a sensible manner.

Monday 2nd March 2015

My section 16 response had to be submitted by the 10th March 2015 and I was still to hear from my solicitor. I decided to give him a call to enquire as to when he was coming to see me. If I was being totally honest, I think that I was more bothered about letting him know that I'd been categorised to a D, despite him advising me that it wouldn't happen until the conclusion of my POCA. When I *did* speak to him, he didn't have a lot to say on the subject of my new category. He did inform me, however, that he'd be coming to see me sometime that week.

In the kitchen, the second grumbler announced that he had quit his job in the visits café. I was sure that there was a moral to that story but held my counsel.

Back on the wing that afternoon and the talk this time was of a new guy who had just moved on that morning. The guy was telling anyone who would listen that he had brought 3ozs of Spice with him onto the wing. That amount of Spice would be worth around £7,500 on the wings of Doncatraz. I didn't give it a lot of thought; probably just prison talk.

I was currently feeling a little fed up with Doncatraz. Nothing had really changed. I think that, knowing I could be moving but not knowing exactly when, was starting to get me down a little. I just wanted to be out of the place now. I spent an hour on the phone with Amy, who was always guaranteed to lift my spirits but, as with all calls, it had to end, then I was back to feeling frustrated. I also had a feeling in the back of my mind that something would go wrong with my transfer and that the promised two weeks could turn into two months.

Wednesday 4th March 2015

Out of habit I checked the ATM machine. As always, I checked my account balance, which was showing a healthy £196.00. I'd break the £200 barrier by Friday – what a result. No matter what, I'd be leaving Doncatraz with more than the £130 I came in with. I checked my timetable, which was showing a visit at 10.00 am. As I hadn't booked any visits, I knew that it had to be my solicitor. I headed off to the kitchen to kill half an hour before the legal visit. I had with me the thick bundle of papers that I'd received in the post four weeks ago. I'd already read through the document a few times and made a few notes here and there. My solicitor finally arrived after half an hour's wait. We trawled through the paperwork relating to my POCA investigation. As I stated earlier, the POCA falls into two parts: The first part is the confiscation order; the second is the benefit figure. The confiscation order is the part that could land you with extra prison time. The confiscation order is the value of all of the realizable assets a criminal has, which may be realized – in other words, any assets that could be sold and perhaps generate a surplus. My solicitor and I had managed to get my realizable assets down to zero. It was all the cash that had been withdrawn from the ATMs in Tenerife that the prosecution were claiming was hidden in a box somewhere. Before my arrest, I had spent time renovating my villa in Tenerife and I had receipts from a builder to prove that this money had been spent. Luckily for me, my builder, in typical Spanish builder fashion, had gotten a little greedy and demanded more and more cash. When I stopped paying him he had left the job unfinished. Now I could demonstrate where the money had gone and, because the work was unfinished, the value of the villa was significantly diminished.

Despite being able to demonstrate a zero assets figure, my solicitor gave me the following advice:

'It's always best to try and give them a bit of something to avoid completely pissing them off; it's all about ticking boxes.'

As with most things, it all comes down to statistics. For example, if the prosecution stuck with their initial assessment of €283,000 (euros) and I failed to pay it, one: it would be recorded as an unsatisfied confiscation order and, two: I would spend more time in prison, at more expense to the taxpayer. Now, if I inform the prosecution that I have £5000 in available assets, the judge would make a confiscation order for that amount. I would pay the £5000, thus causing my confiscation order to be satisfied and saving the taxpayer valuable pounds in board and lodgings at one of Her Majesty's hotels. It would show that the system worked.

In one respect, that is how Chris got somewhat luckier than I did. When he was first arrested, HMRC found £15,000 in used notes in his father's loft. The prosecution took the £15,000 as full and final settlement and did not need to waste money on a full investigation. In the eyes of the law, a criminal procedure had been found and returned back to the state – box ticked.

All things being fair and equal, which they rarely are when it comes to the letter of the law, Chris, like me, should have had a hidden assets figure. But because a box had been ticked there was no point wasting any money on an investigation into Chris as well as me.

If HMRC carried on like this they may be able to increase the number of settled confiscation orders to somewhere north of the 3% mark. We agreed that my solicitor would make an offer of £2000 and then, after negotiation, we would concede to pay £5000. My solicitor just needed the receipts from the Spanish builder, which Amy had filed away and we were good to go.

There was just one slight issue: Jack-an-ory. He was still holding onto a £50,000 charge on one of my properties. The loan relating to the charge had been satisfied a number of years before but Jack-an-ory was refusing to acknowledge this thus causing the legal charge to remain in place. My solicitor advised me that this would have to be reported to the prosecution. Added to this was the fact that a local solicitor who had acted on my behalf during the property transaction also appeared to be acting for Jack-an-ory. This is a big no-no in legal terms and is referred to as a conflict of interest. I was looking forward to seeing how this one unfolded. I was quite surprised that the local solicitor didn't appear to be adhering to the letter of law, especially as one of the partners of the firm was jailed a few years back for his own part in a VAT fraud.

I believe I sidetracked a little… I mentioned earlier the two parts of POCA, so I'll continue in that vein. The second part of POCA is the benefit figure. This didn't seem to worry my solicitor but scared me to death. In my case, as I mentioned earlier, the benefit figure was set at £1.378 million. This figure would not result in any extra time in prison, but would never go away. So, even though I was stating £5000 in assets at that precise moment in time, the benefit figure or part of it could be taken at any time in the future between now and my death. For example, if I won £1 million on the lottery in ten years' time, the prosecution could take it off me. The £1 million would then be deducted from the £1.378 million that I owed. It occurred to me that the reason solicitors do not worry about benefit figures is because by the time it rears its ugly head the solicitor is long gone. I had heard all sorts of horror stories from people who had benefit figures. One guy was left a house by his grandmother, which got taken. Another guy was released from prison, got a job and saved up to buy a new car; the car was taken and liquidated. This next one I found a little hard to believe but I'll relay it anyway. A guy was on his way to Disneyland with his family and he had £5000 in cash on his person. Unluckily for him, he was stopped at the airport and searched. When the cash was found it was taken from him and used to reduce his benefit figure. Scary stuff.

My solicitor informed me that my benefit figure would end up getting reduced to reflect other people's involvement and consequently profit or 'benefit' from the fraud. Luckily, the law had recently changed in that respect. What I'm now going to tell you you will find very hard to believe, but this was a legal fact prior to 2010. Imagine five people had committed a crime and the five people stole or defrauded a total of £1 million. The £1 million would be split up equally between the five, giving them £200,000 each. If those five people were convicted, the law would deem that they each benefited to the amount of £1 million. Each of the five people would have to repay £1 million. So, for a £1 million crime, £5 million would have to be repaid. Luckily, due to the fact that most people who steal £200,000, don't have £1 million to pay back, the statistics started to look bad. The law was then changed and benefit figures became proportional. My solicitor assured me that the benefit figure would at least be cut in half. Even so, I would still be stuck with a figure of around £650,000. So, here's a question for you: Would it be reasonable to expect a person to leave prison with a benefit figure of £650,000 and get a job, pay tax and save money for a car or a house? Maybe that person would feel he had only two choices, a life on benefits or a life of crime. It appeared to me that those people who committed a financial crime were indeed getting punished twice. Food for thought, I suppose.

The meeting concluded and my solicitor promised he'd be in touch soon.

Back on the wing at tea time I was informed about a Spice attack that had taken place on the exercise yard. The guy had collapsed. When the medical response team got to him his heart had stopped. Fortunately for him, the medical team got to him in time and restarted his heart; he was then thrown into his cell to sleep off the effects of the Spice that he'd taken.

Another thing that came up in conversation that afternoon was the pay received by prisoners on wing 3A, the VP or nonce wing. Apparently, any prisoner located on 3A would automatically be paid £15 per week, without having to work for it. The story was that, because they were vulnerable and unable to mix with other prisoners, they were unable to work. Their £15 per week is slightly less than the £17.50 earned by full-time workers but, for me, there was a different issue. There were only 180 full-time jobs available within the prison that held 1130 inmates, so the probability of all 94 inmates of 3A having a job was minimal. Only 15% of the prison population at Doncatraz work, so why should 100% of the 3A inmates earn nearly as much as a full-time worker? Is that really how rapists and paedophiles should be treated?

Thursday 5th March 2015

'Great news, I've had a phone call this morning giving me notice that you're getting transferred to Sudbury in the next 7 days,' announced Bernie as soon as I walked into the kitchen.

I couldn't quite compute what she'd just told me. Seven days and I'd be out of here. The feeling of joy was overwhelming. At last I'd be saying goodbye to Doncatraz. I asked her at least three times if she was winding me up. She assured me that it was all above board. Apparently, and as I knew earlier, the kitchen always got advance notice of transfers to enable them to sort out replacement workers. On top of that, Keith had told me the week before that I'd be gone within two; so it all made sense.

When I entered the library later that afternoon, Clive, ever the voice of reason, told me not to get excited until I was sat on the bus and it had gone through the gates.

While we sat having tea later on, one of the lads, who had been staring at something on the other side of the wing, suddenly spoke up:

'Ay-up, lads, look over there; he's going to have a Spice attack.'

We all looked over to where a youngish lad was sat on a chair next to his cell door. He kept looking around, obviously very paranoid. The next minute the entire colour drained from his face and he went deathly pale. Then the vomiting started. The guy projectile vomited a long stream of brown-coloured liquid. It seemed to go on for an eternity. He paused and then started again. When he could finally vomit no more he gazed around at everyone looking at him and broke into a silly grin. Then he fell forwards and lay in the pool of vomit that he'd just created. No one, including the PCOs, went near him. After around five minutes or so he stumbled to his feet and leaned against his cell door. At this point a PCO ambled over and unlocked his door. Once the guy had fell through it the PCO locked him in and instructed one of the wing cleaners to deal with the vomit. A group of lads stood in the corner of the wing who had witnessed the whole thing continued puffing away on Spice joints completely undeterred by what had just happened. One of the group was the guy whose heart had stopped on the exercise yard just the day before. Ten or fifteen minutes later, bang up was called. The guy whose heart had stopped started to stagger across the wing looking a little worse for wear. When he got to the stairs he put his first foot on the first step and then just toppled over backwards; his head smashed against the hard floor and the blood started to flow. Less than two minutes later the medical response team were taking him off the wing in a wheelchair. It was clear that the rumour about the 3ozs of Spice coming onto the wing was true. I was sure that the weekend was going to be a very interesting one indeed.

Friday 6th March 2015

Friday morning kicked off with someone having a Spice attack in the shower room. There was vomit everywhere. A big cheer went up as the guy who had collapsed in the showers was carried out on a chair by the medical response team. It wasn't even 9.00 am. The rest of the day was pretty normal until I got back to the wing at 5.00 pm. There had been two more Spice attacks on the yard that afternoon. On the table next to ours was a large bearded guy who was rocking in his chair.

'Here we go,' said one of the guys on our table.

A moment later, Beard Face had vomited into his plate of food. The people sat around him who had also been smoking Spice, simply got up and moved to another table. The guy was now coughing violently with more vomit coming at intervals. The smell was disgusting; I was glad that I wasn't eating. We all moved off our table to try to escape the rancid smell. Two PCOs sat on the pool table, watching Beard Face coughing and vomiting; nothing much they could or were willing to do. After it became clear that there was going to be no more vomit, the two PCOs walked over to the guy. He was still coughing in a very unhealthy manner. One of the PCOs put in a radio call to medical response. This was the 18th Spice attack on our wing this week. The interesting fact here is that Spice attacks are only recorded if the medical response team are called. If the PCOs can merely throw the prisoner into his cell, it isn't recorded. The official figure for Spice attacks throughout the prison is ten per week, yet this week there had been 18 on our wing alone. If non-medical response Spice attacks were taken into account, the figure would be in the hundreds.

Saturday 7th March 2015

The PCOs seemed a little more proactive against the Spice smokers today. Anyone seen to be staggering around was immediately locked away in their cell. It was quite entertaining to watch. A female PCO had her eye on a guy who was attempting to do a lap of the wing. He was periodically bumping off the walls as he walked. She unlocked his door, stood to one side and waited as he staggered towards her. Once the guy was level with his door, she gave him a little push, which caused him to stumble sideways through the open door, and swiftly locked it behind him. The only problem with this approach was that when the doors were unlocked again for tea, the smell that came out was overpowering. The Spiced up prisoner would have at least vomited and, in some cases, soiled themselves before passing out.

Sunday 8th March 2015

Church was extra entertaining today. A local eight-piece band came in to accompany the service. Unfortunately, the band outnumbered the congregation 2:1. I was sure it was only six or seven weeks since the group had been in last time. After a chat with the singer, she confirmed that the band only came in every quarter and it was in fact early December when they last performed. Amazing how the time had flown.

The PCOs' proactive attention towards Spice seemed to have worked in so far as there were no attacks openly on the wing. They all happened behind the cell doors and out of sight of the CCTV cameras. Whether or not this was the intention I did not know.

I checked the ATM just before tea and noticed that there was a visit booked for Wednesday morning. I thought that it was odd because I'd already seen the solicitor the week before. I then made the mistake of mentioning the fact over tea. Clive, in his usual serious tone, stated:

'If it's not your solicitor, it's got to be either customs or the police; no one else can visit without your consent.'

Clive had the ability to make the ridiculous sound perfectly plausible. I'd be lying if I said I didn't give Clive's words some thought, but I still managed to sleep soundly.

Monday 9th March 2015

As soon as 8.30 arrived I put a call in to my solicitor to see if it was he who had booked the visit. To my relief it was.

I was killing time waiting for the main door of the wing to be unlocked and got talking to one of the PCOs. He was a friendly chap and very laid back, maybe a little laid back for his chosen career. He told me that he'd be quitting the job soon as he had just passed his HGV test.

'How much do you think we earn in here?' he asked.

I told him that I had no idea. I'd always believed that a prison was one of those well-paid government jobs that came with early retirement and a gold-plated pension.

'Sixteen grand after tax. Sixteen fucking grand for dealing with the shit that we get in here.'

I was quite taken aback. It didn't seem a lot of money considering the shifts that the PCOs worked and the aggravation that they put up with. I could fully understand the guy wanting to quit and turn to HGV driving where he could probably double his salary.

Tuesday 10th March 2015

As I was waiting to be let off the wing for work, a guy stood next to me pointed to a man staggering across the top landing. The man was clearly under the influence of something.

'Look at him Spiced off his tits at 8.50 in the morning he's getting out,' the guy said.

I wasn't sure if he was joking or not. Surely anyone getting released wouldn't be stupid enough to smoke Spice on the morning they were due to go home. Another prisoner confirmed it.

We all stood watching as he tried to walk down the stairs. He managed to get halfway down before he froze. He was gripping the handrail, his legs were twitching but he was unable to move. Two male PCOs who had been watching started towards the frozen guy. As they got closer and started to ascend the stairs, one of the PCOs shouted:

'The dirty bastard's shit himself!'

The two PCOs grabbed an arm each and instructed another prisoner to take hold of the guy's legs.

'We don't want any shit dropping out the bottom of his trackies,' said the PCO.

The three of them, two PCOs and a prisoner carried the guy down the stairs and to his cell. The door was already open so the PCOs simply threw the guy onto his bunk to sleep it off while lying in his own faeces. The cell door was promptly locked behind him. I heard that the guy was still released later that day despite the fact he had to be carried to reception on a chair by two PCOs.

When I arrived at the kitchen for the second day running, there was no sign of my sidekick, Bones. Bernie put a call in to his wing. The wing staff informed her that Bones had been caught with a mobile phone in his cell and was now on basic regime for 28 days. He also faced outside charges, which could result in additional time being added to his sentence. The penalty for possessing a mobile could be up to six months' additional prison time. If the police could establish that the phone had been used for criminal activity the added time could be even greater.

I spoke to a lad who was on the same wing as Bones and he told how Bones managed to get caught with the phone. Apparently, some guy on the outside had been making improper advances on Bones' girlfriend. Bones had phoned the lad on his illegal prison mobile phone and told him in no uncertain terms to keep away from his girlfriend. The lad had then made a report to the prison that he was getting threats from an inmate. Security had then entered his cell at 11.30 pm and found Bones lying on his bunk with the mobile phone next to him. Unfortunately, this would also result in Bones losing his job in the kitchen. I was quite disappointed at this as Bones was a laid back guy who was easy to work with. He was also pretty good at the job, so now, for the time being, I was flying solo in the sweets section again.

Wednesday 11th March 2015

Another legal visit and, if I am being honest, it was something I quite looked forward to. I had the impression that my solicitor was enjoying himself now that he suspected that local solicitors who had been dealing with my property sales were appearing to be not completely honest. I also guessed that the problem caused by the local solicitor was enabling my guy to rack up a few extra hours in legal aid.

'I've requested a copy of the conveyance file from your solicitor, but I wouldn't be surprised if a certain amount of filleting had taken place,' explained my guy.

I was a little taken aback; surely a solicitor wouldn't remove information from a file to cover his own back.

I also still had the problem with Jack-an-ory, which my solicitor was also dealing with. This was also covered by legal aid. I have to say that prison was turning out to be rather productive. Over the hour-long session, statements were prepared along with an action plan for my local solicitor and for Jack-an-ory.

Thursday 12th March 2015

I was still expecting to be transferred to Sudbury the next day, as it would be the final day of the two-week time slot I had originally been given. I thought I'd better double-check, so I asked Keith to put in another call to his mate and chase it up for me. The news wasn't good. The story that was passed to me was that Sudbury was unable to give confirmation of a place for me. They would try and resolve it next week. I knew that there had to be more to the story than that. When I got to the library later that afternoon it became a little clearer. Chris was in the library talking with Amanda, our caseworker. She was explaining to Chris that although he had been re-categorised to D at the same time as me, his computer file had not yet been updated and wouldn't be until sometime next week. This got me thinking: maybe whoever was responsible for transfers had decided to wait until Chris was on the system as a Category D prisoner, then they could send us to Sudbury at the same time. Of course, this was only an assumption on my part but, now, understanding a little of how the prison worked, it certainly made sense. I had the feeling that this could delay matters far beyond next week and I have to say that I was feeling utterly dejected. Over the past two weeks I had gotten used to the idea of getting out of Doncatraz and moving to somewhere nicer. Now that had been snatched away and here I was, a category D prisoner stuck in a category B prison.

Friday 13th March 2015

I woke as usual at 6.45 am to breakfast television. I was feeling somewhat disappointed that this was supposed to be the day I was going to Sudbury, but instead was remaining here in Doncatraz for the foreseeable future. I decided that there was no point dwelling on the matter; what would be, would be.

When I arrived in the kitchen, Bernie informed me that I would have someone new with me until I was transferred. This was so the person could get used to making the sweets before being left on their own. Thankfully, she gave me the option to choose who could come and work with me. Most of the lads in the kitchen were decent, although there was no one whom I really wanted to work with. There was, however, a YO (young offender) who had only just come into the kitchen and was currently on pots. He had shown a little interest during the week in what I'd been making, so I decided that he would be as good as anyone. Levi was only 20 and was on remand for theft. His crime was more to do with foolishness than anything else. Levi's story went something like this:

Levi had been out one night in his car and had run out of petrol. Apparently, he decided to look in the garden shed of a nearby house for a jerry can. On opening the shed door he didn't find a jerry can but a fancy motorbike. His rationale was that, as he was going to steal a jerry can, he may as well steal the motorbike. That was exactly what he did. Needless to say, he got caught and here he is on remand at Doncatraz.

Levi was very keen although a bit on the inexperienced side, especially when it came to matters of hygiene. I will give just one example of his slightly unhygienic ways:

We had just made a batch of scones and I asked Levi to dust them with icing sugar. He was a little heavy-handed with it to say the least and had dusted far too much on. When I pointed this fact out to him, he told me he'd sort it out. I don't know what I was expecting him to do but it definitely wasn't what he did next. He bent down and starting blowing the icing sugar off the scones. I could see tiny flecks of spittle landing on the dusty scone tops and leaving little damp splodges. To make the scenario worse, he'd been coughing all morning and had told me he was recovering from flu. Levi couldn't understand why I threw the scones into the bin.

Sunday 15th March 2015

The Fall Guy returned from his morning visit looking a little stressed and upset. He told us the following story:

'Everything was going well on the visit. The wife was in good spirits and even the lad was quite chatty, well, as chatty as a 16-year-old lad was going to be. He was wearing one of my old coats and looked quite grown up. Towards the end of the visit my son went off to the toilet but didn't come back. About ten minutes later a PCO came over and told my wife that she needed to sit with my son while the police interviewed him. When he'd returned from the toilet, a PCO had done a random search and found a SIM card in the pocket of the coat.'

The Fall Guy was one unlucky guy. Because the SIM had not been detected when the lad had entered the prison, it would be assumed that The Fall Guy had passed it to him on the visit. To bring or attempt to bring a SIM or mobile phone into or out of prison is a criminal offence. That was why the police had been called in to interview The Fall Guy's son. According to The Fall Guy, the SIM card had been in the coat for months. He'd put it there one Saturday before he was imprisoned. He and his son had been out shopping and The Fall Guy had taken out a new phone contract for his son. The lad had wanted to use the new SIM right away so The Fall Guy took out the old SIM and put it into his coat pocket. Little did he know that months later his son would wear his coat to visit him in prison. Talk about unlucky. He was convinced though that once the police analysed the SIM card, they would discover that it had not been used for any criminal activity or even used at all for the past few months. The problem that The Fall Guy now faced though was not a police problem. It was a prison problem. In the eyes of the prison, whether a SIM card had been used or not was irrelevant. The point was that a SIM card was contraband and the prison had a zero tolerance policy on this. He was told that he would be notified of the outcome of the prison in due course. That little phrase seemed to crop up everywhere. The Fall Guy's immediate problem was his job. He was a Catch 22 orderly, which allowed him access to all wings within the prison. If he was considered a security risk he would lose his job. The Fall Guy was a very trusting sort of chap and was convinced that his female boss was a decent sort and wouldn't sack him. Myself and a couple of others tried to tell him that, although he wouldn't be convinced that just because staff were friendly did not mean they were your friends. When it came to the crunch they would do little to help you out.

Just before tea that afternoon, I headed off to the shower room. Chris and Clive were using two of the cubicles and there were two other guys sat in the room on plastic chairs smoking. Judging by the smell coming off the roll-up cigarettes, they contained a little more than just tobacco. Again, as I have complained earlier, I found it most disagreeable that someone could be in a confined space smoking, while other people where trying to get clean.

Around half an hour later, during tea, I began to feel a little sleepy. Considering it was only 4.30 in the afternoon, this struck me as being odd. That was until Chris and then Clive said that they were also starting to feel drowsy. We soon came to the conclusion that whatever the other guys had smoked in the shower had affected us too. We had all been subjected to passive Spice smoking while taking a shower – the joys of prison.

Monday 16th March 2015

Another typical day in Doncatraz. When I started work in the afternoon, I asked Keith to call his mate again and see if he knew any more about my transfer. The news wasn't too inspiring. I was told that I definitely would not be moving this week but that I would definitely be moving sooner rather than later. Better than 'moving in due course' I suppose.

I spoke to my father that evening who had been dealing with the local solicitor on my behalf. I wanted notes of the meeting that had taken place a year or so before between the solicitor, Jack-an-ory and I. The solicitor was saying that he had no recollection of the meeting. The words of the criminal solicitor came flooding back – 'filleted file'. Surely this couldn't be the case. Was the local solicitor really trying to hide the fact that he'd met with Jack-an-ory and me, thus causing a conflict of interest? I was sure my legal solicitor would enjoy this latest twist.

Wednesday 18th March 2015

'Ten minutes to bang up!' shouted the PCO.

It seemed extra noisy on the wing this evening and I was quite looking forward to getting locked away at 6.00. There was a sudden movement on the top landing near to my door. A small group had gathered and one of them shouted out for a PCO. I joined a few others in moving a bit closer to try and see what was going on. Lying on the floor in the middle of the group was a prisoner. To protect his identity, I will call him Paul. Paul was lying motionless except for a twitching of his left leg. At this time there were only two female PCOs on the wing. One was older and experienced but the other one was very young and relatively new to the job. The two PCOs rushed to Paul's side. The younger one was looking pale and extremely shaken.

'Get to your doors,' shouted the older PCO.

Locking away 94 prisoners who wanted to stay out and watch the drama was a slow process. Having only one PCO doing the locking away, while the other stayed with Paul, made it even slower. By the time I was finally locked away, Paul had been put into the recovery position and was vomiting. A classic sign of a Spice attack. A couple of minutes after my door had been locked, I heard the medical response team come onto the landing.

'He's flat lined,' said one of the nurses.

There then seemed to be a flurry of activity and I guessed they were using a portable defibrillator. At this point, I couldn't see what was happening but I could hear most of what was being said. There were some urgent whispers and then I heard another nurse say:

'Just nod if you can hear me, Paul.'

I heard him vomit again, so at least they had managed to start his heart. At 6.30, Paul was still on the floor but still not responding to simple questions.

'Paul, tell me your prison number.'

A grunt followed.

I later found out that Paul's heart had stopped a total of seven times while he lay on the landing floor.

'We've got another one!' shouted the younger PCO from the ground floor.

I heard one of the nurses swear before running along the landing and down the stairs to attend to the other Spice victim.

The time was approaching 7.00 pm and Paul had been down for over an hour.

'I've never known one to be out for this long,' said one of the medical team.

From my cell window, I noticed an ambulance pull into the car park at the front of the prison.

'Paul, tell me how old you are.'

This time he managed to answer.

'Fir'y-nine,' slurred Paul.

The next thing I heard the nurse say made me laugh to myself.

'Jesus – 39. He's either still off his tits or had a bloody hard life.'

She was right, though. To look at Paul you would guess that he was in his late 40s or early 50s. Maybe I shouldn't really comment, as no one would believe that I was 38, although I kept telling myself that this was because I obviously looked much younger.

A couple of minutes later, two paramedics came onto the wing and stretchered Paul off to hospital.

Thursday 19th March 2015

When I got to the library that afternoon I was told that there were yet another two Spice attacks on our wing that day. I considered two attacks in one day to be pretty unremarkable, however, my opinion changed when I found out who one of the Spice attack victims was – Paul – the guy whose heart had stopped seven times. He had been discharged from hospital in the morning; by lunchtime he was smoking Spice again and then collapsed in the exercise yard.

Later that day over tea, The Fall Guy told us that he had received a response to the comp 1 form regarding his categorisation. As with Chris and I, The Fall Guy had also been awarded category D status at his initial categorisation meeting, only to have it changed to a C Category by the countersigning officer. However, as with most things relating to The Fall Guy, luck was not on his side and the C categorisation had been upheld. The comp 1 reply stated that he was not eligible for category D status until he had served more time in prison. We discussed this amongst ourselves over tea and, as a result, The Fall Guy decided to submit a Comp 1A form. A Comp 1A form is used when a prisoner is not happy with the decision returned on a Comp 1. The personal superior to the officer deals with this who countersigned the ICA1 form. After all, there is nothing in the categorisation guide that states a prisoner has to spend a certain amount of time as a particular category or in a particular prison.

Friday 20th March 2015

Yet another legal visit; my third in two weeks. My guy was defiantly making the most of the legal aid system. My solicitor had been to see my father to discuss a statement regarding my assets. We spent time discussing various aspects of the POCA investigation and then moved onto two letters that he had drafted and which needed approving. The first one was a letter to Jack-an-ory, giving him a final opportunity to come clean and prevent himself getting dragged into a full-scale financial investigation of his financial affairs. My solicitor seemed to think that anyone with the slightest bit of intelligence would not want their finances scrutinised by any government organisation. I had the feeling that Jack-an-ory would ignore my solicitor and take his chances. Time would no doubt tell. The second letter was my favourite; it was to the local solicitor asking him to provide answers to a lot of questions that would probably make him feel very uncomfortable. His response would determine if we had a case to report them to the Solicitors Regulatory Authority.

Later on, during service in the kitchen, I was chatting to one of the PCOs from 1B when a security officer walked over and handed him a large brown envelope.

'What's that; a bribe?' I asked.

'No, it's a piss test kit. A couple of us on the wing think we may be suffering the passive-smoking effects of Spice, so we're going to see if the piss test can confirm it,' replied the PCO.

This made sense and, in a way, confirmed the sleepiness I'd felt last Sunday. If the staff, who were never in confined spaces with smokers, were feeling the effects, then it stood to reason that inmates who *did* share confined spaces such as the showers, would be affected too.

I really hoped that the PCO tested positive. It could make the prison take a closer look at its duty of care policy for both staff and inmates. It was plain to see who the users of Spice were and most of the PCOs also knew who was dealing it, yet no action was ever taken. In fairness to the PCOs, they were unable to take any action unless the dealer was actually caught in the act but this would be virtually impossible. I could not understand, however, why no harsher action was ever taken against the users. I decided to put the question to a PCO, who responded:

'I've given up nicking the Spiceheads because of all the paperwork involved.'

A 'nicking' was the term for an internal prison charge that would lead to both negative comments on a prisoner and a punishment. The punishment could be up to 28 days on basic regime and, in some extreme cases, outside charges by the police. To issue a nicking involved filling out reports and in some cases taking statements and so the PCOs tried to avoid them at all costs. The result of this was a general lack of discipline and respect. In the four and half months I had spent in Doncatraz, I'd only witnessed one person on basic regime for 28 days. According to the PCO, basic regime caused its own problems.

The basic regime was as follows:

- Banged up for 23½ hours per day
- Half an hour on the exercise yard but not with any other prisoner
- Meals to be eaten in the cell
- One shower every 72 hours but not in the company of others
- Television set to be removed from the cell.

I will now demonstrate how the basic regime was *not* adhered to. Due to staff shortages it was not possible to have a PCO supervising a single prisoner on the yard, so a prisoner on basic exercised with everyone else. Standard prisoners receive one hour's exercise; therefore, as the basic prisoner was exercising with everyone else, he too would get the full hour. Again, it would need an additional PCO to escort the man on basic back to his cell after 30 minutes. To provide meals in the cell, a PCO would have to go to the servery and carry the meal to the prisoner's cell.

Again, there were not enough staff to carry out this duty so the man on basic would be let out along with everyone else at mealtimes. In theory, the man should fetch his own food and return to his cell, but this was never the case. The problem was the same with showering. Men on basic would be let out not only at mealtimes but also in the morning for a shower. It was not unusual for the man to be let out again for a shower in the afternoon, as he would simply state that during the morning shift he had not been let out for a shower. The removal of the television set was another non-event as most of the cells were double and it was unlikely that both occupants of the cell would be on basic. The television would have to stay for the benefit of the prisoner *not* on basic. The final insult to the basic regime was the lack of communication between the PCOs. If a prisoner was put on basic regime by a particular PCO, it would only last until that PCO took a day off. The covering PCO would never check the list to see which prisoners should be on basic, so the duty PCO would unwittingly let the prisoner out as usual. I would like to point out that I am not intending to have a go at the PCOs. I am merely stating what most PCOs would agree with. The problem is not with the PCOs' ability to carry out their duty, but the small number of them expected to do he job of many more.

Saturday 21st March 2015

Saturday yielded the usual game of poker in the morning. One of the lads who also worked in the print shop and thus had time on his hands had made up some poker chips out of some thick card and printed values on them. They were quite rudimentary but were a definite improvement on matchsticks. We looked quite professional now with a green cloth and circular chips. For me, poker was the making of the weekend. Eight lads sat around a table having a game of cards and a laugh. It is the one thing I will defiantly miss about Doncatraz. I ended up winning the game, which meant I would not need to buy any biscuits for the next two weeks. Great result.

There were the usual Spice attacks on the exercise yard, but today seemed a little different. Usually the Spiceheads would throw up and collapse, but the three victims today suffered violent shaking followed by paralysis. One guy, who was carried in from the exercise yard by two prisoners, was completely rigid. His feet were dragging on the floor as the other two struggled to carry him. The thing that struck me was his face. He looked like he had been frozen at the time of receiving some very shocking news. His unblinking eyes were wide and his mouth open yet unmoving. He looked more like a manikin than a living person. It took five minutes to manoeuvre him to his door, during which time he didn't blink once. Another guy on the yard had simply gripped the fence and was shaking as though it was electrified. This carried on for ten minutes before the Spice had worn off and he'd returned to circling the yard with everyone else.

Monday 23rd March 2015

The Fall Guy submitted his comp 1A form regarding his categorisation. This had been done with the help of the unofficial prison solicitor, who now believed that there were at least 100 prisoners who had an incorrect category. I was interested in The Fall Guy's situation. In my case, it had only taken the submission of a comp 1 to rectify my categorisation, yet this had not worked for him. The comp 1A was the next stage in the complaints procedure and would be dealt with by a senior manager. There was, however, a downside for The Fall Guy. The senior manager was a woman who had a reputation for disliking decisions to be challenged that were made by her department.

As I left for work I spoke to Chris who was going to have a word with the lady from IMB. She would perhaps be able to find out some information regarding our move to Sudbury. We agreed to meet up once I'd finished in the kitchen.

I met with Chris at around 2.00 pm. He'd spoken to Lynne from IMB earlier and she was now in the Catch 22 office chasing our move. Although Lynne had sounded positive, she had advised Chris against pestering the Catch 22 department.

'They may just send you anywhere and not where you necessarily want to go,' were her words of warning.

This seemed ridiculous to me as Doncaster had a policy to try and locate prisoners back to their home areas. This policy had come from the director and had been reiterated at the weekly PIAC meeting in February by Mr Pete Cooper from Catch 22. From what I could see, the policy was not getting implemented; I was coming up to five months inside and was still 70 miles from home. I knew a guy in the print shop who was from Scotland. He had been battling since October to be sent closer to home and yet he still remained here in Doncatraz. Chris had also met a guy that morning that had been waiting for eight months for his move. My mind flicked back to what a guy had said to me when I first arrived:

'This is a pretty good jail but bloody hard to leave.'

How very true. Lynne soon returned to us and the news was short but sweet:

'You two are definitely on the next bus to Sudbury.'

That was all they would tell her. The term 'next bus' implied to me that there were buses leaving the prison all the time. In fact, no one that I'd spoken to, neither prisoner nor staff could recall a bus ever going to Sudbury. As Lynne left us, Amanda arrived.

'Tweedledum and Tweedledee – just the men!' grinned Amanda.

She explained that she was intending to come and find me. Amanda confirmed that all OASys assessments carried out after the 5/1/15 had to be followed up with a 'monthly chat'. The 'chat' was to assess a prisoner's ongoing progress.

'So, everything is still okay? No problems?' she asked.

'No, I'm not okay; I'm still here,' I replied, trying not to sound too bitter.

'You two are on the next bus out of here. As soon as there's enough people to fill a bus to Sudbury, you'll be on it.'

We chatted for another couple of minutes. Amanda then scribbled something on her clipboard and left. I doubted that she noted anything about my dissatisfaction at still being here at Doncatraz.

When I returned to my room there was a slip under my door.

'VIDEO LINK - TUES 24th MARCH - 2.00PM'

It took me a moment to realize what it was for, then I remembered that the 24th March had been set by the judge as a hearing to finalise my POCA. I recall thinking at the time that the 24th March seemed a long way off and yet here it was. How time flies when you're having fun. I knew that due to the local solicitors and Jack-an-ory, we were a long way off reaching any sort of agreement. The court appearance would only serve to set a new date and would last less than two minutes. Even so, there would still be a full legal team line-up consisting of my solicitor, my barrister, a solicitor and a barrister for the prosecution, including the usual vast array of court staff. It's a good thing that it is not illegal to waste public money.

Tuesday 24th March 2015

I finished work in the kitchen a little earlier than usual so I'd be on time for my video link. I headed over to house block two where the video link room was situated, for my court appearance. I wondered why the whole thing couldn't be done by video link. The judge could stay in his chambers and the barristers in their offices. I was grateful, however, that I was dragged off to court in person, so this would certainly save a few extra quid. I was directed to level three by a PCO and when I arrived I was locked in a large holding room while the link was established. The room contained a few comfy chairs and some outdated copies of the *Daily Mirror* – not my first choice of reading material. A couple of minutes later a PCO led me from the holding room and into another room that was partitioned into two booths. There was a small flatscreen TV in each booth, along with a chair in front of the TV and a set of headphones resting on the top. The PCO directed me to booth number two.

'Sit down and put the headphones on,' he instructed before leaving the room.

I put the headphones on and looked at the blank screen, not quite knowing what to expect. A few seconds later, the screen flickered to life. My solicitor and a guy wearing a wig, who I presumed was my barrister, filled the screen. A small box in the bottom right-hand corner of the screen displayed my face. The barrister introduced himself and explained that the purpose of the hearing was to ask the judge for additional time. The one addition he made was that the prosecution had put forward a deal:

'Make us a sensible offer regarding your UK assets and we'll forget about your overseas assets.'

I laughed when he told me this.

'My thoughts exactly,' replied the barrister.

We all knew that there was no equity in my overseas property portfolio and the prosecution did not want to spend any money investigating the fact, so in reality it was a non-offer. I had to admire the guts of prosecution for making such a ridiculous offer. I decided that I'd have to repay the favour at some point.

'So, may I presume that you would like me to refuse the prosecution's offer, Mr Lowndes?' continued the barrister.

I confirmed that this was indeed my wish and the video call ended. The PCO who must have been watching from elsewhere, returned as soon as the screen went blank.

'Okay, back in the waiting room for a few minutes.' He led me back to the waiting room. No sooner had I just sat down and reached for a newspaper when the PCO returned. This time I was taken to a larger room. There was a bigger flatscreen television, maybe 40 or 50 inches at one end of the room. At the other end was a desk and chair facing the television. The PCO directed me to the chair behind the desk before sitting down on a chair next to the door, as if guarding it. The screen came to life and the inside of a courtroom was displayed. The clerk of the court made the introductions as the camera panned to each face, one by one. The final image was that of the judge. To my relief, it wasn't the vicious lunchtime drinker who had sentenced me. The judge asked me to confirm my name before the prosecution stood to address the court. The camera zoomed out to give a full view of the courtroom. The prosecution barrister began by detailing the funds that the local solicitors had been holding for the past four months. He requested that the funds be transferred to my legal solicitor's client account until matters had been resolved. My barrister immediately agreed to this. The prosecution could have asked for a restraint order to be placed on the funds; this would have attracted various costs, so this was a small victory on our part. If the local solicitor had acted correctly there would be no funds to restrain or even transfer. The prosecution were aware of a property sale that had taken place in December 2014 and were happy for the funds to be distributed, as I deemed necessary. However, thanks to the incompetence of the local solicitor, the prosecution had effectively received a windfall. I was pretty sure that I would not be seeing the money again.

The next part was straightforward. The prosecution and defence both agreed that more time was needed and a new timetable was set out. The 26th August 2015 was earmarked for a day-and-a-half mini trial, should an agreement not be reached beforehand. The hearing concluded and the screen went blank. A total of 6 minutes 32 seconds, start to finish.

Wednesday 25th March 2015

Before I went to work I called my solicitor. I wanted to hear again why my money, which had spent four months sat in the local solicitors' client account, now had to spend another five months sitting in *his* client account. In all honesty I knew why – I just wanted someone to lose my temper with. Since it was only 8.30 am and the local solicitor didn't open for another half an hour, I had to settle for my solicitor. After a five-minute rant I felt considerably calmer before hanging up – a pound of phone credit well spent.

When we finished work in the kitchen that afternoon, Steve was waiting in the corridor and began searching people. The first lad he searched had two pieces of cold chicken breast stuffed in his underpants. The guy was instantly sacked. He tried to reason with Steve in saying that the chicken wasn't for him but for his mate on the wing. Why anyone would want cold, uncooked chicken that had come from someone's underpants I will never know. Regardless, the dismissal stood. Steve had also discovered two small boxes containing cakes, stashed in the changing room, so he knew that there was at least one other person stealing from the kitchen. The problem for Steve was that, unless he caught the perpetrator, there was nothing he could do. I could understand how frustrating this must have been for

Steve. Whilst we worked in the kitchen we could eat whatever and as much as we wanted, yet some people would still want more. I had to wonder whether it was the actual food or just the thrill of stealing that appealed. On the other hand, it could just be habit.

Thursday 26th March 2015

Over tea, The Fall Guy told us about his 'interesting' meeting with Kerry, the manager of Catch 22. Kerry was the person responsible for dealing with his Comp 1A complaint regarding his categorisation. Comp 1A forms are usually dealt with in writing so it was quite unusual for the manager to summon a prisoner in person. There were rumours that anyone who got summoned by Kerry was in for a dressing down. I'd put this down to prison lore; that was until I heard The Fall Guy's story, which went something like this:

'Kerry sent me a message saying that I had to report to her immediately. It felt a bit like getting summoned to the headmaster's office at school. 'Sit down' was her unfriendly greeting as I entered her office.'

"I believe you are questioning the ability of my staff to do their job," she began.'

'I was just about to try and explain that that was not the case but she cut me off mid-sentence.'

"I haven't finished! What do you think gives you, a prisoner, the right to question us on our decisions?"

'Her tone was condescending to say the least and decided it best not to reply; however, she continued:'

"I demand to know who put you up to making this complaint and to challenge our authority."

'I told her that no one had put me up to it and that I just felt that I should be a cat D prisoner.'

"You committed two offences whilst on bail – you are a category C prisoner – end of story. Now, I trust this will put an end to this matter."

'I was then dismissed, feeling like a chastised schoolboy.'

The Fall Guy seemed visibly shaken as he recounted the events of the meeting. I was shocked by the story. Catch 22 was meant to be a professional organisation. I was well aware that the Catch 22 staff appeared to know very little about prison law, although I thought they could at least attempt to hide their ignorance behind a veil of courtesy and professional attitude. I don't wish to bore you with prison law so I will try and keep this simple.

As I have set out earlier, categorisation is determined by a nationally adhered to algorithm. There are three sections: A, B and C. Each section contains a series of questions to which the answer is a simple 'Yes' or 'No'. In order to be categorised a D cat prisoner, all the questions in sections A and B must have been answered as 'No'. In section C, it is permitted to have a single 'Yes' and still be granted category D status. One of the questions in section C, the one that The Fall Guy answered 'Yes' to, was:

'Were there any offences committed whilst on bail?'

The guidance note states that, even if a number of offences are committed they only make up one 'Yes'.

In the case of The Fall Guy, there was a public order offence and a drink driving offence. The former was an argument he had with his accountant in a public place. It was non-violent; just a case of raised voices and some pushing and shoving. However, it was on a high street late in the evening and a police officer happened to be present, resulting in a caution. The drink driving offence is self-explanatory. It must also be noted that The Fall Guy was on bail for a total of five years. These two offences still only added up to one 'Yes' on the algorithm, which meant that he should have been a category D prisoner. For reasons still unknown to me, Catch 22 felt they had the power to ignore the nationally used categorisation document and categorise prisoners according to their own set of undocumented rules. According to the unofficial prisoner solicitor, there were over 100 cases of mis-categorisation at Doncaster. He was currently working closely with IMB to put together a report for the Ministry of Justice. In conclusion, the Fall Guy had every right to appeal his categorisation decision and Kerry had absolutely no right to speak to him about and certainly not in the manner that she did. There was one last hope for The Fall Guy and that was to complete a Comp 2, which would go directly to the director of the prison. No doubt the director would take the time to read the documents that governed his prison. I doubted whether The Fall Guy would be keen to take this option though.

The one positive, at least for the rest of us that came from this episode, was the opportunity for a good wind up. As it was April Fools' Day on Wednesday, we thought it would be a good idea to post a ship out notice under his door. The plan was to locate a prison in the most remote part of the country and put the details on a ship out notice. One of the lads was always let out early in the morning to drop off milk and cereal packs, so he could push the slip under The Fall Guy's door early in the morning. As I worked afternoons in the print shop, I had access to the templates to make the ship out notice look authentic. In the meantime we just needed to do a little groundwork.

'The last person to get on the wrong side of Kerry got shipped out the following week,' Clive casually commented.

'Wasn't it somewhere out of the way? Bristol or somewhere,' I asked.

'Kent rings a bell.'

'She hasn't got the power to do that, has she?' asked The Fall Guy, clearly taking the bait.

'Well, not wanting to worry you, but no doubt time will tell,' was Clive's response.

Friday 27th March 2015

Friday morning was normally the best day in the kitchen. Steve would bring bacon from the main kitchen, so it was bacon sandwiches all round. However, due to there still being a thief at large, Steve announced:

'You can fuck off if you lot think you're getting bacon sandwiches this week.'

I'd noticed over the past couple of weeks that the wing was taking a turn for the worse. One of the PCOs who ran the wing with discipline and commanded a level of respect had been on sick leave for a few weeks. This appeared to be having a detrimental effect on the overall running of things. The PCO in question was ex-military and, along with one of the better female PCOs, would regulate who came onto the wing. They would ensure that there weren't too many lads from either Doncaster or Barnsley on the wing, as this would always end up with gangs being formed. Their policy seemed to be 'divide and conquer'. They tried to maintain a mixture of men from lots of areas along with, when possible, older and more mature prisoners. During my time on wing 1B, this policy had worked well and the wing was generally calm and well behaved. There was the odd incident but this was more the exception and not the rule. The drugs were always there but the threat of disturbance and violence was not.

For the past couple of weeks, with the decent female PCO having been on annual leave, combined with the ex-military PCO on sick leave, the wing was losing its calm. The wing was filling with the type of prisoner who enjoyed a little disorder. 'Donney Lads' were getting their mates transferred from other wings onto 1B, as were the 'Tawn Lads', lads from Barnsley. Many of the PCOs would agree to this for a quiet life. Two clear gangs had now emerged on the wing. The general noise level on the wing had increased, as had childish acts such as throwing food. The one thing that really did annoy me was at night when prisoners would shout to each other from behind their doors. The shouts would always be the same, starting with 'Yo' and ending with 'Bruv'. For example, 'Yo, Tony, can ya lay on some burn, Bruv?', which roughly translated, means 'Excuse me, Tony, would you be kind enough to lend me some tobacco?' The thing that would baffle me most was that everyone was locked up until morning, so nothing could be exchanged, borrowed or purchased. Why not just wait until morning, walk up to Tony and ask him quietly to his face as opposed to bawling across the wing and disturbing my enjoyment of the evening television?

I later learnt that things could be borrowed or exchanged using 'lines'. If a prisoner on the top landing wanted to borrow something from the guy on the landing below him, he would cut a strip of his bed; this was known as a line. He could then attach a roll up to the line and hand it out the window. The person in the cell could then catch hold of the line and pull it into his cell window. Items could also be set upwards in the same way.

Saturday 28th March 2015

As was becoming the norm now, 1B was short-staffed. Two female PCOs left to supervise 94 adult male prisoners. Luckily, everything remained calm, unlike 3D where a single inmate had run riot. He'd ripped the hot and cold water pipes off the wall in the laundry room, causing a flood. The tumble dryer and washing machines had then been tossed over the railings from the first to the ground floor and the dustbins had been set alight. In the end, the Tornado squad had to be called in to resolve the situation. The Tornado squad is a police unit that specializes in prison riots. It took a full six hours to restrain and then detain the guy.

That afternoon, as I hadn't been unlocked for work in the library, I pushed the call button. Ten minutes later my door was still locked, which was not unusual. I shouted to one of the wing cleaners walking past my door and asked him to call me a PCO.

'There's no one on the wing, Bruv,' responded the wing cleaner.

There were at least 15 prisoners walking around the wing and no PCO to supervise. I knew that one was on the exercise yard but that still left the other one unaccounted for.

That night there was the usual shouting and door banging. At around 9.30 pm there seemed to be some extra loud screaming coming from a cell somewhere on the top landing. I could hear a PCO running up the stairs and along the landing towards the cell. The next thing I heard was the PCO radioing for urgent medical and security back-up. I later established that the cell belonged to the guy who had vomited into his dinner the previous week. He was an avid Spice smoker and had decided to take a razor blade to his arms and face. When the security team opened up his cell to disarm him, he could be heard screaming about aliens taking over his body. He was using the razor to try and cut the aliens out of his arms and legs. The guy was finally calmed down and taken off to healthcare to be patched up. This type of behaviour was not unusual for Spice smokers. A PCO from another wing had told me about a couple of other instances of self-harm induced by Spice. One man had tried to remove the skin from his arm while another one had taken to biting lumps of flesh from his arms and eating them. The PCO believed it was down to the psychosis effects caused by Spice.

Sunday 29th March 2015

When we were unlocked on Sunday morning, I noticed a mop and bucket on the landing outside the cell of the slasher. It had obviously been used to clean up the blood from the night before, but no one had bothered to move it. The bucket was yellow and the mop blue, indicating that it should only be used in food preparation areas. I would be prepared to bet that the mop and bucket would be returned to the food serving area. Finally, at 1.00 pm, 16 hours after the incident, the bloody mop and bucket were removed from the landing. What I didn't see, however, was where they were returned.

The one productive activity for the day was continuing to plan the wind up of The Fall Guy.

The wing was typically noisy and the atmosphere seemed particularly tense; I wasn't sorry when bang up was called ten minutes early.

Monday 30th March 2015

I was feeling a little fed up Monday morning, which was unusual as, normally the start of a working week was a positive thing. I put it down to the fact that I was now a category D prisoner stuck in a category B prison with no indication of when I may be transferred. I decided to go and see Amanda. My plan was to ask her if I could be transferred to the next available cat D, regardless of location. I had come to the conclusion that my chances of getting a transfer to Sudbury were virtually zero. I figured that if I could get to a local category D prison, I could apply for a transfer to Sudbury from there. Chris was of the same opinion, although for him there was a slight gamble involved. Chris was due for ROTL (Release on Temporary Licence) on the 3rd August 2015. This meant that he would need to be in his final prison no later than the 3rd May 2015. The reason for this is that a prisoner cannot leave a prison for ROTL before completing a 12-week 'lay down'. After the 12-week lay period, so long as a prisoner has reached his ROTL date, which is the 25% point of his sentence, he is then eligible to spend unsupervised days out of the prison. These days could be spent at home and at work. Our understanding was that Chris would need to spend 12 weeks at Sudbury before he would be permitted at ROTLs. So, the gamble for Chris was this; did he spend four more weeks at Doncatraz and hope to be transferred directly to Sudbury? Or did he try to get to a local cat D and be moved from there within the next four weeks?

When I got to the Catch 22 office, I was informed that Amanda was no longer my caseworker. In future, if I wished to speak to anyone, I would have to submit an App.

Over lunch in the VT kitchen, I sat next to a guy who had just begun work there. He had spent the last ten years in and out of various prisons including category Ds. We began chatting about different prisons and the differences between categories. What he told me was a big help. According to the guy, the 12-week 'lay down' period applies to Category D prisons in general and not to the specific prison. So in essence, if you spent six weeks at one Category D prison and then moved to another, you would only have to wait a further six weeks to complete the 'lay down'. So, in the case of Chris and I, any Category D would suffice. We could go to a local category prison and then would have 12 weeks to get transferred to Sudbury. I was suddenly feeling a lot happier. All I needed now was for Catch 22 to transfer us to the next available category D prison.

As I left the prison, I bumped into Chris and The Fall Guy. The latter was now a Catch 22 Orderly and told me that I had been allocated to his caseworker, Chloe. The bonus was that The Fall Guy worked in the same office as Chloe. The offices were also in a different part of the prison, a part with no locked doors. I could now forget about submitting Apps and just walk into the office to see her. I decided that there was no time like the present so headed off in search of Chloe. We were told that she was in a meeting but were welcome to wait. A few minutes later, Mr Pete Cooper, the Catch 22 manager, entered the office.

'Well, I'm surprised to see you two still here; thought you'd have been shipped out weeks ago,' was his greeting.

'So did we, Pete. You wouldn't know anything about a transport to Sudbury, would you?'

'I've heard a rumour that there may be one going soon.'

The man should be a politician with a response like that; talk about an evasive answer.

'We were thinking about going to a local Cat D and then getting a transfer from there. What do you think about that, Pete?' asked Chris.

'To be honest, I don't think that would get you to Sudbury any faster.'

With that, he disappeared into one of the offices. A few moments later Chloe joined us. She explained that as I had only just been allocated to her, she hadn't read my file and knew nothing about my circumstances. She also told me that tomorrow was to be her last day before two weeks of annual leave. I gave her a quick rundown of the situation and that I would be happy to go to any cat D prison. She said that she'd make some enquiries and told me to return the following afternoon. Chloe had a reputation for doing her utmost for prisoners, so I left feeling relatively happy.

Monday tea time, there seemed to be a lot of tension on the wing. It reminded me of how 1A was when I first came here; a constant underlying tension and feeling that things could erupt at any minute. A few of the tables that were usually separated had now been pushed together so all the factors of one various gang could sit together. Another group of around ten prisoners had congregated in a corner of the wing. This was the sort of behaviour that would normally be associated with YOs; not what one would expect from fully grown adult males. Bang up was finally called without incident. That night there was more shouting and door kicking than usual.

Tuesday 31st March 2015

Tuesday morning bore yet another legal visit. My solicitor informed me that we had to devise a strategy. He described the whole POCA process of being quite like a game of poker, quite apt really, although as he put it:

'The prosecution have nothing, yet everything to gain, whereas you have everything and therefore everything to lose.'

Comforting words. My solicitor gave me an example of how things could go. The prosecution were alleging that I had €200,000 (euros) hidden in Tenerife. I had answered the allegation by providing receipts that the €200,000 had indeed been spent. In my opinion, that should have concluded that particular argument. But if it went to a hearing, the judge could rule that the receipts were fakes. After all, I was a convicted fraudster so the court is not obliged to believe anything I say or any evidence that I submit.

'Couldn't we just fly the builder over?' I suggested.

'I'm coming to that.' The solicitor explained that, if I wanted to take the gamble of a hearing, he would call as many witnesses as possible. He would first, though, have to fly to Tenerife along with a translator for a couple of weeks to have all of my assets independently valued and to locate potential witnesses. Then he would have to arrange for the witnesses to be flown to the UK for the duration of the hearing. All of this sounded very expensive, which of course it would be. Fortunately, legal aid would be picking up the tab so ultimately the bill would land with the taxpayer.

'Although, the problem is that the judge may decide not to believe the builder, he may think you paid him a bribe to testify; after all, you are a convicted fraudster,' continued my solicitor. I seemed to be hearing that final sentence a little too often. Once upon a time I had believed that justice was blind and that courts and judges take a balanced view. This belief was fast eroding.

'In POCA cases, the judge is merely an agent for the state,' the solicitor stated.

What wonderful news. We did a few rough calculations and, if I took this matter all the way and lost, the judge could make an order against me for around £500,000. I would then be given six months to pay and, if I failed to do so, I could face an extra five years in prison. The best-case scenario was that I would pay £1 and serve no extra time. That was the gamble with the hearing option. There were two further options: Number one was to make an offer now, wait for a counter offer and then try to meet somewhere in the middle. Option two was to plan for the hearing and then hope the prosecution made a sensible offer at the 11th hour as, according to the solicitor, the prosecution would not want the expense of running a hearing.

I decided to make an offer there and then and if the prosecution declined it I would move to the hearing option. As was my normal morning routine, I had checked my prison account balance on the ATM. I had a few pennies over £240 in my spending account.

'Okay, John, my offer is £240.00. Take it or we go for a hearing.'

'You want me to go to the prosecution with that?'

'Indeed I do.'

So, that was settled. I wasn't quite sure if my solicitor thought I was being serious or not. I would love to see the prosecution barrister's face when he heard the offer.

There still remained three other issues. Number one, the biggest, was the benefit figure. POCA didn't stop with assets that a criminal held at the time of the crime. The law was furnished with another weapon to trust into the wallet of the criminal, the 'benefit figure'. I'll give an example of how this works. In my case, the prosecution state that the value of the crime that I was involved in along with others, was worth £1.378 million. This was despite the fact that I was sentenced on £1.8 million. How the figures were calculated I didn't know but on this particular score I was not going to argue. If all my current assets were sold and raised £300,000, this figure would be deducted from the value of the crime, so there would be a balance of £1.078 million. This would be the 'benefit figure' and can be collected at any point in the future for the rest of my life. I detailed the consequences of this earlier.

We now had to persuade the prosecution that the £1.378 million should be proportioned between the people involved in the crime. In my case, there were three people charged and three people found guilty; therefore, it should be sensible to request a three-way proportion, although the split would not be equal. My solicitor seemed to think that the prosecution try to allocate 50% to me. This still meant a figure of roughly £690,000 minus whatever was raised through the sale of any assets I may have.

I had spoken to a few people on the wing that had been through the POCA process. The general consensus was that the benefit figure was the final bargaining chip. So for example, if the prosecution wanted £100,000 from me, I could agree not to fight that figure if they would agree to a zero benefit figure. I did doubt whether this would really be the case. My solicitor informed me not to give too much thought to the benefit figure. He assured me that even if I was handed one, it was unlikely to ever be enforced, as it was a costly exercise to keep checking up on bank accounts and assets. Unlikely wasn't really good enough for me; I would be much happier with a zero benefit figure.

The second issue was how to deal with the local solicitor. The news here was a little more encouraging. There were two forms of complaint that could result in me getting compensated for any money I'd lost due to their negligence. We agreed to pursue the complaint once the POCA issue was settled.

The third issue was Jack-an-ory. He still had not responded to any correspondence from my solicitor and still needed to be dealt with. My solicitor suggested a hitman, which I have to admit was quite appealing. I was confident that if I held a whip-round in the local area I would have no trouble paying for the best hitman available.

'I was joking,' added the solicitor, disturbing me from my fantasy. After a little more discussion we decided to make a police report regarding the threats of blackmail and see how he responded to that. If a hearing *was* to take place he would also have to appear before the court as a hostile witness – more fun and games.

I left the legal meeting feeling confident that everything was in hand. My only problem now was how to get out of Doncatraz. I headed off to find Chloe to see if she had any news on the subject. When I got to see her, the news wasn't good.

'No one knows anything. You'll have to wait until this time next week. The man in charge of transfers is off until then.'

To say I was gutted was an understatement. Another full seven days before I'd stand a chance of finding anything out.

I spent the afternoon working on the wind up that we had planned for The Fall Guy. Clive had found the address of a prison in Kent, so I was busy adding the details to a mocked up transfer form. The end result looked very convincing. Maybe forging official prison documents wasn't the wisest way to spend my time in prison, but as my solicitor kept reminding me, 'you are a convicted fraudster'.
As a little hint that the document might be a fake I signed it from 'Assistant Director, Joe King'. Perfect.

When I arrived in the library that afternoon Clive told me that the unofficial solicitor had been put on that day's ship out list. Fortunately for him, he was only on the reserve list. He was, however, down on the main list for the coming Thursday. In normal circumstances, a manager could veto the decision to transfer a prisoner. For example, if the prisoner was on an education course or doing a specialist job, their transfers could be put on hold. Some prisoners were happy to stay in B cat prisons where they had a good job and in many cases, a single cell, rather than move to a C cat where they would return to a double cell and initially no job. The other reason that some prisoners would rather stay in Doncatraz was the money. The unofficial prisoner solicitor did two jobs and earned £105 per week. In the local cat C, which was government run and not private, his wages would be reduced to around £11 per week, a significant pay cut. The decision to transfer the unofficial solicitor had come from director level and therefore could not be vetoed by a manager. It seemed obvious that the decision to transfer him was political. The help and guidance with categorisation decisions and appeals were obviously not appreciated by the powers that be. It seemed quite a coincidence that earlier this week, the Ministry of Justice had been in the prison and had spoken with the unofficial solicitor and discussed at length about 'the fundamental problems with the allocation and categorisation of prisoners at Doncaster'. It had been suggested that the reason Chris and I were still stuck at Doncatraz was because we had the audacity to appeal against our categorisation decisions. I would never know whether that was actually the case or not.

We spent the half hour evening mealtime winding up The Fall Guy, telling him he would definitely end up somewhere unpleasant now that he'd upset

Kerry. In all fairness to him, he took it all in his stride.

Another particularly noisy night on the wing; more and more people seemed to be joining in the shouting as the week progressed. Fortunately, by around 9.00 pm, the shouters had shouted themselves hoarse.

Wednesday 1st April 2015

The day of the wind up. Clive was out early as usual dropping the tea packs outside the cell doors. He managed to slip the brown envelope containing the fake transfer document under The Fall Guy's door without the PCOs noticing. When our doors opened at 8.00 am, The Fall Guy didn't emerge. Chris, Clive and I were stood on the landing opposite trying to see into his room, without success. Around 15 minutes later he appeared and trudged over to us, his head bowed slightly. I felt a twinge of guilt as he approached and told us that he was to be transferred to the other end of the country.

'I'd half expected it, after how Kerry spoke to me,' he managed to say before retuning to his cell.

We decided to leave it until lunchtime and then break the news that it was a hoax. On the way to the shower room, I passed by The Fall Guy's cell. I peered in to see him sat in a chair with his head in his hands. I couldn't leave him believing he was going to be transferred to Kent, so I popped my head in and asked to take a look at the transfer document. He handed it over without looking up.

'Assistant Director, Joe King!' I read out loud.

The realization hit him as the words left my mouth.

'You bastards; I knew it was a wind up!'

Luckily, while he shouted a few expletives, he was still smiling. Chris and Clive had joined us now and we all had a laugh about it.

Thursday 2nd April 2015

I'd just walked out of the shower room when The Fall Guy wandered over and offered his hand.

'I'm getting transferred, mate.'

I shook his hand and then broke into a grin. I realized he was trying to get his own back for the day before.

'Thought you'd be a bit more original than that, old boy.'

He swore that it wasn't a wind up. After a couple of minutes and finally showing me the documents that definitely weren't fakes, I believed him. He was getting shipped to the local C cat prison that very morning. To me, this was proof that management didn't like to be questioned. The poor guy had followed the correct procedures in questioning a decision and had gotten shipped to another prison for his trouble. There were a couple of positives for The Fall Guy. The first was that the C Cat prison where he was going was a state run prison so he may stand a better chance of getting his cat D status from there. His appeal process should, in theory, follow him to his next prison. Hopefully, people without any ulterior motive would review it. It was quite possible that The Fall Guy could end up in cat D before me. The second positive was that he would be on the same bus as the unofficial solicitor, so at least he was going with someone he knew.

Over tea that afternoon, a group on the table next to ours were chatting loudly about a documentary that was on the TV the previous night. The documentary was about the riots and rooftop protests that had taken place at Strangeways prison in Manchester some 20 years ago. I hadn't watched the documentary myself, but from what I heard it should have made everyone imprisoned at Doncatraz feel very fortunate indeed. However, a lot of the men, I use that term very loosely, who had made their way onto 1B recently, lacked the brain capacity to understand what it meant to be fortunate. In fact, many of them found it difficult to even use a knife and fork, so logical thought was a bit of a stretch, as the following brief exchange I overheard will demonstrate:

'A riot id be sick, innit, Bruv?' *(A riot would be a most enjoyable experience. Don't you agree, my good man?)*

'Standard. I'd be up for ripping da tiles off da roof.' *(What a splendid idea. I would love to remove the tiles from the roof)*.

If the simpleton had bothered to look out of his cell window he would have noticed that Doncatraz did not have a tiled roof. The roof was pressed steel, but maybe I'm just being picky. The guys were basically looking for any reason to kick off. A few minutes later it came. The washman came out of his cell and headed towards his gang. He was shouting, using a lot of expletives and using the word 'Bruv' a lot as he walked. I managed to gather that his daughter was ill and he was unable to speak to her on the phone. The reason he couldn't call his daughter was because his ex-girlfriend had requested the prison remove her phone number from his approved list. It was quite a common thing for a prisoner's ex-girlfriend or even current wife or girlfriend to request that the prison prevent a prisoner from making contact via phone. Some prisoners can get quite paranoid while locked up and begin believing that their partners are up to no good. After this jealousy has festered for a while, the prisoner will end up placing abusive and threatening phone calls to the female in question at all times of the day and night. This was the case with the washman, so he was now no longer in a position to contact his ex-partner. He wanted the PCOs to allow him to use a prison phone in one of the offices where the call bar would not apply. Naturally, the PCOs were not willing to allow this breach of protocol.

'We'll refuse bang up, until 'e get 'is phone call, innit?' suggested the wing Spice dealer.

His little gang of followers thought this was a great idea. I don't believe for one minute that anyone cared about the washman's plight. If the washman himself was really concerned about speaking to his daughter he could have used the mobile phone that he had stashed in his cell. This wasn't about phone calls; it was about making an excuse for confrontation with the staff.

'Five minutes to bang up!' shouted a PCO.

The whispers began to spread around the wing:

'We'll refuse bang up till he gets his phone call.'

About 60 prisoners moved to one side of the top landing and gathered in a tight huddle leaving about 30, myself included, who moved to stand by our doors. The PCOs began locking away those of us who were stood by our doors. Two PCOs then walked over to the group of 60 *'hard men'*. As I suspected, they were all-talk. Thirty minutes later everyone was locked away without incident or even a raised voice. Once everyone was locked away the bravado returned and the shouting that evening went on until well past midnight.

Friday 3rd April 2015

Friday was the first day of a four-day weekend, which meant no work and the weekend regime. It was going to be a long haul. As it was Good Friday, the church was showing *The Passion of the Christ* on a big screen, so at least that was a chance to get off the wing for a couple of hours. At 9.00 am my door was unlocked by one of the few decent PCOs:

'What are you still doing here? I thought you'd have been shipped out by now.'

The PCO had been on leave for the past two weeks and had already wished me luck before she left, fully expecting me to be transferred in her absence.

'I really didn't think I'd still be here either, but that's Doncatraz for you.'

'They've certainly let some shit onto the wing while I've been off. It's only a matter of time before something big kicks off.'

She was right; the wing seemed to be deteriorating by the day. It seemed a lifetime ago since wing 1B was one of the best wings in the prison with zero violence and very few visible drug problems. The laid-back atmosphere had completely disappeared now. In reality it was only during the past three weeks that things had begun to go downhill, but when you're surrounded by shit, time goes much slower.

Three of us headed off to church at 9.30 to watch the film or, in reality, to get off the wing. I had heard about the film but had never seen it before and have to admit it was quite a graphic film. At 11.30 the film finished and we were ready to go back to the wing for lunch. We were told by one of the PCOs in the church that we must stay put for the time being as there had been a disturbance on 1B. It was another half an hour before we were permitted to leave the church and return to the wing. When we returned to the house block and towards our wing, we saw two female PCOS standing outside the wing door. The younger of the two who was relatively new looked white as a sheet and was staring at the floor.

'I've not seen anything like it in all my time here,' said the other PCO as we approached. She had worked at Doncatraz for the past eight years, so this was quite a statement.

'They're fucking animals. Five of them all laid into one man,' she continued.

She unlocked the wing door and led us in.

'Get straight to your doors and keep quiet, we're on lock down,' she said in a whisper.

There was tension in the air as I walked slowly to my door; some of the other inmates began kicking their doors and shouting. I felt relieved to be locked away. The big question now was how long would we be locked down for?

Sunday 5th April 2015

Sunday morning we were finally unlocked after spending around 45 hours locked down. Food was eaten in our cells with no exercise or showers despite it being Easter Day. This was typical prison punishment – a few idiots cause a problem and all 94 men on the wing are punished. It did give me a good chance to do plenty of writing though, so it wasn't all bad. The talk on the wing was the incident on Friday. Apparently, it had started in a row over a game of pool. A guy from Sheffield had been playing a game and a guy from Doncaster decided that it should have been his turn to play. The Doncaster guy had decided it was worth fighting over, but unfortunately for him, the Sheffield lad soon got the better of him. At that point, four of the Doncaster lad's mates decided to join in and they turned on the Sheffield guy. He was beaten with a pool cue and, once he hit the floor, another *'Doncaster hard man'* decided to administer a few kicks to the head. With five men kicking and punching him, the Sheffield lad didn't stand much of a chance. At the time, there were only two female PCOs on the wing and they knew better than to get involved. By the time the back-up staff had arrived from other wings, the Sheffield lad was in a bad way. He was rushed off to hospital and three of the five Doncaster lads were removed from the block and put into solitary confinement. The atmosphere on the wing remained pretty tense, with a lot of staring going on between the factions from Sheffield and Doncaster. Again, I was not sorry to be locked away again after lunch. I gave the afternoon association a miss and instead dedicated the afternoon to writing. I had now gotten to the stage where I had very little interest in spending any time out of my cell and on the wing. I think it was probably a combination of the tension and the fact that I knew I should be sat in a category D prison and not stuck here in a B cat holding prison.

Monday 6th April 2015

Monday was another bank holiday and the last day of the weekend regime. At least I had a visit that afternoon and that was always something to look forward to. I spent the morning writing and then at 1.15 pm got off the wing and headed off to the visits area. As I sat in the waiting area, I began chatting to an older guy. He told me that he was only serving 6 weeks and did so at the same time every year. He went on to explain that he was not a believer in paying council tax. So, each year he refused to pay it and each year he was jailed for 12 weeks, released in six, for non-payment.

'As I see it, it's a double whammy. I don't have to pay the bill and I get six weeks' board and lodgings at the taxpayer's expense,' he explained proudly.

My name was called and I went down the stairs into the main visits area. I handed over my ID card, was fingerprinted and then allocated a table number. I walked over to the table and waited for my visitors. A few minutes later my partner and parents entered the visits hall. The hour-and-a-half flew by as usual. I asked my dad if he would give Sudbury a call to ask them if they currently had space and were accepting prisoners. As my visitors left, I assured them that this was the last time they would have to make the long journey to Doncatraz.

'We'll see,' were my father's parting words.

Tuesday 7th April 2015

I awoke feeling like a bus had hit me. My whole body ached. I decided a day in bed was the best solution. My cell was unlocked and relocked around six times during the day; for exercise, lunch, association and tea. The PCOs didn't quite understand that I wanted to be left alone to feel sorry for myself.

Thursday 9th April 2015

I didn't move from my bed until Thursday evening, when I managed to go down for tea and eat a single apple. I was sure I'd be back to normal by morning. I gave my dad a quick call to see if he had called Sudbury for me. Apparently, the person he'd spoken to couldn't confirm one way or another whether they were currently accepting prisoners but did say that the prison wasn't full and hadn't been for over a year. This gave me a bit of something to take to my caseworker, although whether it would make a difference was anybody's guess.

Apparently, that morning, while I was still recovering in bed, one of the guys who had served 8 months in Doncatraz and was due to be released in two weeks, had been transferred to a Cat D prison. As has happened before and as mentioned previously, I couldn't see the point in this exercise. There would be very little to gain from the prisoner's point of view.

Friday 10th April 2015

I got up that morning feeling more or less back to normal and decided it would be best to go to work. I'd gotten sick of the sight of my tiny room. After a busy morning in the kitchen, I headed off to the print shop for the afternoon. Keith, the manager, was waiting for me.

'Have you heard?' he asked as I walked in.

I had no idea what he was talking about. He told me that I was to be transferred to Sudbury category D prison on Monday. I was ecstatic; it didn't feel real. I asked Keith if he could check to see if Chris was getting transferred at the same time. It only took him a couple of minutes to confirm that this was indeed the case. Keith then told me to take the afternoon off.

'A chance to get things sorted for your move' was Keith's reason, although I suspected that Keith didn't really want any prisoner who knew he was getting transferred, to be around the computers and equipment. I could fully understand his reasoning.

I set off to try and locate Chris and give him the good news. I finally caught up with him in the library where he had already been informed about our transfer by the librarian. We were both in very high spirits, although to me it still didn't feel real. Once I got back to my room I made a couple of phone calls; first to my partner to give her the news that I was soon to be a great deal closer to home and then likewise to my dad.

Sunday 12th April 2015

The weekend was dragging by. My mind was firmly fixed on the transfer and what could go wrong. I had this feeling of dread that the transport would be cancelled or break down and that I'd end up stuck here for even more time. I attended church to try and occupy my mind but it didn't really work. I was unable to concentrate on writing either, so spent the time watching mind-numbing TV.

Monday 13th April 2015

I awoke at around 5.00 am, feeling like a child on Christmas morning. I would not be unlocked for another three long hours. I decided to begin packing up my belongings. I was surprised at how many things I had managed to accumulate during my short stay in Doncatraz. I had extra clothing, books and piles of letters and paperwork, including a few certificates. It only took around ten minutes to pack so I resorted to watching some early morning TV. Finally, my door was unlocked at 8.00 am. I headed off to the showers for the last time at Doncatraz.

'I've just heard all buses to Sudbury have been cancelled!' shouted Clive from the end cubicle.

I returned his comment with some good-natured expletives. After my shower, I met up with Chris and we went to find a PCO to enquire as to the time of our departure. We were told we wouldn't be going anywhere until at least 11.00 am. We decided to kill the time by going down to the kitchen to say our goodbyes to Steve and Bernie. We spent nearly an hour drinking coffee and generally wasting time, then after a handshake from Steve and a 'good luck' from Bernie, it was back to the wing. Time seemed to have slowed down; it wasn't yet 10.00 am. There were also a few handshakes and 'goods lucks' received from various guys on the wing. It was a common thing amongst prisoners to be pleased for anyone who was going to somewhere better, even if you barely knew that person. At around 10.30 am, one of the PCOs told us to collect our things, as we would take a steady walk to reception.

The PCO who had unlocked me that morning walked us down to reception. Before going through to the reception area we shook hands, thanked her for everything she had done to make our lives that little bit more bearable and promised that we would not be back. The goodbye felt a little awkward; in a way I felt that someone who had made my first time in prison a little easier deserved more than a stiff handshake, although I suppose it cuts both ways because, during my time here at Doncatraz, I had not caused any problems for the staff and so therefore their time too was maybe a little easier. The door to the reception area was unlocked and relocked behind us. I walked to the same counter that I had stood at some five-and- a-half months previously and handed over my ID card. There were various forms to be signed, which only took a few minutes. I was then directed to the goldfish bowl-style waiting room while Chris went through the same process. I picked a book from my plastic bag and began reading; Chris joined me a couple of minutes later. After ten minutes a PCO entered to ask if we wanted an early lunch and were told to help ourselves to tea from the trolley outside. Remembering how bad the tea was when I first arrived, I decided to give it a miss.

At 11.30, two officers wearing GeoAmey uniforms entered the reception area. Our names were called and we followed them to a waiting secure transport identical to the one that had brought us from the court. Chris and I were the only two occupants on the bus and we were soon secured in the little telephone box-sized cubicles. The engine started and the bus slowly rolled towards the gate - a pause while the gate slid open and the bus rolled slowly through it. That was it, I was out; I glanced out the window to see Doncatraz for what I hoped to be the last time. Next stop - Sudbury. The big question was: what would the next 18 months hold for me?

ALSO BY CRAIG LOWNDES

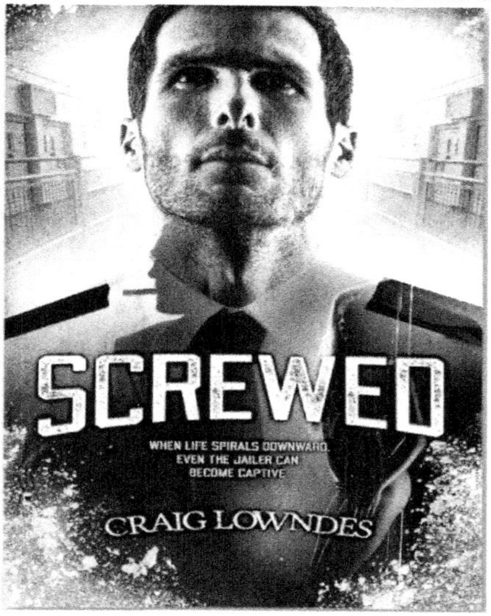

Prison Officer Ian 'Gilly' Gilmore is an ordinary man with an ordinary life. That was until a chance encounter with a sultry blonde in a local bar took his life in a whole new direction.
Seduced by a lifestyle of champagne, VIP bars and exclusive parties, Officer Gilmore soon finds himself in the unenviable position of having to do 'favours for favours'. His newly adopted nickname of Razor couldn't be further from how Gilly feels as his life spirals out of control and into the murky world of drugs, corruption and murder.
How long will it be before the jailer becomes the captive?

ALSO BY CRAIG LOWNDES

Officer James Dimmock, chief investigator at Customs and Excise fraud unit has only two things in his life. His job and his car. He also hates to lose.
When a diligent assistant bank manager accidentally discovers a multi-million-pound VAT fraud, Officer Dimmock can't wait to add another scalp to his 'trophy cabinet'.
But will it be that simple? Has Dimmock finally met his match when he tries to capture Thomas 'Fergie' Jenkins and his band of fraudsters.
The odds are stacked against Dimmock as he battles against corruption and murder in his pursuit of justice.

WWW.LEEKAUTHOR.CO.UK

Coming soon……

Sutlins

A prison Diary
Volume Two

Spring 2018

Printed in Great Britain
by Amazon

36848639R00209